## MACMILLAN

A Simon & Schuster Macmillan Company
1633 Broadway
New York, New York 10019-6785

Library of Congress Cataloging-in-Publication Data

Crocker, Betty.

[Chinese low-fat cooking]

Betty Crocker's Chinese low-fat cooking.

p.   cm.

Includes index.

1. Cookery, Chinese. 2. Low-fat diet—Recipes. I. Title.

TX724.5.C5C76            1995

641.5'638'0951—dc20        95-35415

CIP

ISBN 0-02-860391-5 (alk. paper)

## GENERAL MILLS, INC.

Betty Crocker Food and Publications Center

Director: Marcia Copeland
Editor: Karen Couné
Recipe Development: Susan Rasmussen, Lisa Golden Schroeder
Food Stylists: Kate Condon, Katie McElroy

Nutrition Department
Nutritionists: Elyse A. Cohen, M.S. and Nancy Holmes, R.D.

Photographic Services
Photographer: Steve Olson


Cover: Iris Jeromnimon
Book design: Michele Laseau/George McKeon

For consistent baking results, the Betty Crocker Kitchens recommend Gold Medal flour.

You can create great-tasting food with these approved recipes from the Betty Crocker Kitchens.
Cooking and baking have never been so easy or enjoyable!

Manufactured in the United States of America

10  9  8  7  6  5  4  3  2  1

First Edition

Cover Photo: Emperor's Shrimp (page 69)

# Betty Crocker's

# CHINESE LOW-FAT COOKING

MACMILLAN • USA

# CHINESE LOW-FAT COOKING BASICS

Chinese cooking fits very well into today's American lifestyle. The characteristic ingredients of Chinese dishes—lean meat, poultry and fish, crisp vegetables, rice and noodles—match our growing taste for lighter yet nutritious foods. The one element in Chinese cooking that goes against this concept is the amount of oil used for stir-frying, deep-fat frying or to just make the food look shiny. Reducing the amount of oil and other fats in Chinese cooking is what this book is all about.

There are no hard-and-fast rules with low-fat Chinese cooking. You can be as creative as you like, with no limit to the dishes you can prepare with the fresh produce you can find in most markets. You need no special equipment, just a few sharp knives, a spatula or two, plenty of bowls and a good nonstick skillet or Dutch oven, if you don't own a wok.

It does take some time to prepare recipe ingredients, but very little time to cook them, and in the end, the result is something that pleases all the senses. Chinese food is pleasing to the eye because it has attractive color and shape. It is fragrant with the aroma of fresh ginger, lemon or garlic; it contrasts sweet and sour, hot and cold, and smooth and crunchy. None of these qualities are lost when reducing the fat in your favorite foods.

The ingredients listed here are available in supermarkets or in Asian specialty markets in most cities. And, many of the dishes use frozen vegetables or prepackaged produce you probably already use.

## LOW-FAT COOKING

Traditional Chinese cooking embraces three basic methods: cooking in oil (stir-frying or deep-fat frying); with water (steaming); or with dry heat (roasting, which is done mostly in restaurants, as few Chinese families have the right sort of ovens in their homes). Let's take a closer look at the methods used here (we have eliminated deep-fat frying, for obvious reasons).

**Stir-frying.** Stir-frying cooks food in a small amount of oil over high heat. Ingredients are added in a specific order and are stirred vigorously over high heat so that everything is cooked at the same time. By using nonstick utensils and cooking spray, we have greatly reduced or eliminated the oil for stir-frying. Many woks are available with nonstick finishes. Look for utensils that won't scratch the coating, like hard plastic spatulas or large wooden spoons. A well-seasoned rolled carbon steel, aluminum or stainless-steel wok may also work well without oil.

When using nonstick cooking spray, never spray directly onto a hot surface as it will burn. If more spray is needed for the next stir-frying step, always cool the wok slightly before spraying. Because nonstick cooking spray tends to burn easily, our recipes are cooked over medium-high heat.

Before beginning to stir-fry, it is important to read the recipe completely and to measure and prepare all ingredients. Assemble ingredients in the order in which they will be used. Remember that tougher ingredients such as broccoli require longer cooking times and should be added first, while tender ingredients such as mushrooms require less time and should be added last. It is easy to tell when stir-fried food is cooked because it changes color. Thinly sliced chicken and pork turn white and beef is no longer pink. Vegetables are a brighter color but are still crisp.

When stir-frying, make quick, downward strokes to keep the food moving. Use a spatula with a firm base, slip it down the side of the wok and across the bottom, turning the food over. Use one hand to stir and the other to hold onto the wok. If any food should stick, wash, dry and respray the wok between steps as you cook.

**Steaming.** Steaming is used for meats, fish, poultry, dumplings and rice. Traditionally, food is placed in a bamboo steamer, which is covered and set in a wok. Boiling water is added to just within 1/2 inch of the bottom of the bamboo steamer; the steamer is covered and then heated. (The amount of water used in our recipes will produce steam over high heat in about 15 to 25 minutes.) You can also use a metal or wooden rack placed in a wok, Dutch oven or electric skillet as a substitute for the bamboo steamer. Place the food on a heatproof plate or bowl on the rack and cover the plate with a tight-fitting lid that will allow for the steam to circulate in the one or two inches of air space above the food.

You can improvise a steamer or rack by using empty cans, inverted heatproof bowls or chopsticks in the bottom of the wok, Dutch oven or skillet. Place the food on a heatproof plate and set the plate on the empty cans. Fill the wok with boiling water to within 1/2 inch of the top of the cans and inverted bowl or to within 1/2 inch to the bottom of the plate and cover the plate tightly. Be sure to check the water level during steaming; add boiling water if necessary, but pour it down the side of the wok so that it does not touch the food.

**Blanching.** Blanching is the brief immersion of vegetables in boiling water to partially cook them. Blanching preserves their color, texture and flavor. To blanch, place prepared vegetables in a wire strainer with a long handle; lower the strainer into boiling water and cover. Tender vegetables such as Chinese pea pods should be blanched approximately 30 seconds, or until the water returns to a boil. Tougher vegetables such as broccoli and cauliflower may take up to two minutes. After the vegetables have been removed, they should be rinsed under cold running water to stop the cooking.

# CUTTING

Traditionally, the Chinese try to achieve "harmony of cut," whenever possible. This means all the ingredients are cut in the same way. If the main ingredient of a recipe is shredded, then so are the other ingredients.

It is very important to know how to cut correctly. Your cleaver or knife should always be clean and very sharp. The hand holding the food should always have the fingertips hold the food securely on the cutting surface, with fingers curled so the knuckles almost touch the knife's blade. The knuckles act as a guide for the blade. Gradually move the hand back while cutting. It is a safe guideline not to lift the cutting edge of the blade higher than the knuckles of the hand holding the food unless the fingers are safely out of the way.

**How to Cut Safely**

**Diagonal Slicing**

*Keep the blade at an angle to the cutting surface.*

## Slicing Meat

*It is easier to slice meat that has been in the freezer for about 15 minutes or just until it is firm but not frozen.*

## Slicing Celery and Bok Choy

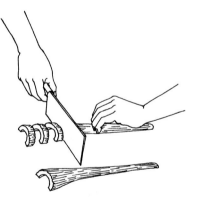

*Cut straight across at the widest end of the stalk.*

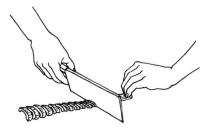

*Cut across the stalk at an angle as the stalk narrows.*

## Dicing and Cubing

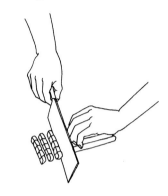

*Cut meat or vegetables into strips less than 1/2 inch wide for dicing, wider for cubing. Hold strips together and cut into pieces as long as they are wide.*

## Shredding

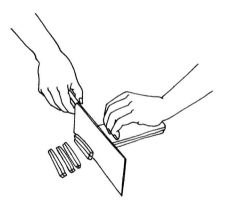

*Cut meat or vegetables into 2 × 1/8-inch slices. Stack the slices; cut lengthwise into thin strips.*

## Roll Cutting

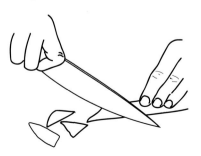

*Keep the blade at an angle to the cutting surface. Roll vegetables such as carrots, zucchini or asparagus one quarter turn after each cut.*

**Green Onion Flowers**

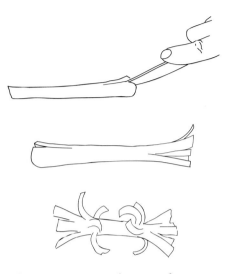

*For each flower, remove root and green top from 1 green onion. Cut white part of onion into 3-inch piece. Make 4 lengthwise (parallel) cuts about 3/4 inch deep into one end; repeat on other end. Place onion in iced water about 10 minutes or until ends curl. Drain on paper towel. Use as garnish.*

**Green Onion Brushes**

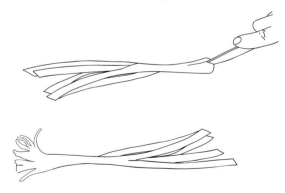

*For each brush, remove root from 1 green onion. Make 4 lengthwise (parallel) cuts about 3/4 inch deep into white end of onion. Place onion in iced water about 10 minutes or until end curls. Drain and shake off excess water. Use to brush on sauces.*

# CHINESE UTENSILS

It isn't necessary to purchase any special utensils to prepare low-fat Chinese food. You can easily use the same nonstick cookware and nonscratch utensils used for everyday low-fat cooking. A few sharp knives, skillets, saucepans, a Dutch oven, turners and strainers are all you need. Cookware for low-fat Chinese cooking includes:

**Chopsticks.** Chopsticks are known as "quick little ones." They are used for eating, cooking and stirring ingredients, and they are said to represent extensions of the thumb and first finger. Plastic, lacquered or ivory chopsticks are used for eating, while bamboo and wooden ones are used for cooking (they don't bend or melt from the heat as the others do). Different in shape from Japanese chopsticks, Chinese chopsticks are longer and less tapered, with blunt tips.

**Spatula.** The spatula used by the Chinese has a long bamboo or wooden handle and a slightly curved edge which fits the shape of the wok. With its slight lip, the spatula can hold sauces. A plastic pancake turner works just as well in a nonstick wok or skillet.

**Ladle.** The ladle is shallow and bowl-shaped, with a long bamboo or wooden handle. It is used to remove food from woks, but a large serving spoon is adequate.

**Wire Ladle and Strainer.** The wire ladle is really a wire mesh scoop with a long, flat bamboo or wooden handle. It is used primarily to remove food from broth or oil. A plastic slotted spoon works just as well in a nonstick wok or skillet.

**Cleaver.** Cleavers come in different sizes. The most useful has a blade three to four inches wide and about eight inches long. Large, heavy cleavers ("bone knives") are used to chop meat, including the bone; few Chinese preparations call for the meat and bone to be separated. Thinner cleavers are used to slice meat and vegetables.

**Steamer.** Traditional Chinese steamers are made of bamboo. They are shaped like round baskets with woven bottoms and lids and rest on the curved sides of the wok. When reheating, more than one steamer may be stacked in a wok. When steam cooking, don't stack. Steamers vary in size from four inches in diameter, for cooking dim sum, to sixteen inches in diameter, for cooking seafood and poultry. A ten-inch diameter steamer is the most versatile.

**Wok.** Woks were designed for stir-frying, to shorten cooking time and save fuel. They are an all-purpose cooking utensil, perfect for deep-frying, steaming or stewing food.

The wok easiest to use is fourteen to sixteen inches in diameter. Woks are made from rolled carbon steel, aluminum or stainless steel. There are also electric woks and woks with nonstick finishes. The carbon steel woks are the traditional Chinese versions. They were developed to heat quickly and evenly and to save fuel; they require special care. To "season" a carbon steel wok, wash it with hot, soapy water and dry it on your stove over medium heat. Rub about two teaspoons of vegetable oil evenly over the inside of the wok, using a soft cloth. Repeat the process if food sticks during stir-frying.

Aluminum and stainless steel woks require no seasoning, but they do not heat as evenly as carbon steel. Because they do not rust, they are a good choice for steaming foods. Electric woks are also convenient. Be sure to follow the manufacturer's directions for their care and use.

# TIPS FOR LOW-FAT CHINESE COOKING

Healthful eating and exercise habits are extremely important in the pursuit of a healthful lifestyle. One overriding dietary concern today is the amount of fat we eat. High blood cholesterol is a major risk factor for coronary heart disease (CHD), our nation's number-one killer. And more than any other dietary factor, saturated fat in the diet can raise our blood cholesterol levels. Less fat also means fewer calories—an extra incentive to keep our fat intake down.

- Use nonstick cookware and nonstick cooking spray to decrease or eliminate the amount of oil needed in cooking. Many woks are available with a nonstick coating. You may also find that a well-seasoned rolled carbon steel, aluminum or stainless steel wok can cook foods without sticking.

- Cut the amount of fat or oil in a recipe by one-half. If you get good results, keep reducing the fat until you find the minimum amount that will produce an appealing dish.

- Avoid fried and otherwise fatty items, such as deep-fried chow mein noodles, egg rolls and traditional sweet-and-sour dishes. We have developed new techniques for achieving the crispy texture we like so much in many of these dishes. You'll be pleasantly surprised with the recipes for Baked Lemon Chicken (page 34), Egg Rolls (page 17) and Sweet-and-Sour Chicken (page 44).

- Serve chicken, turkey or fish. Light-meat chicken and turkey are naturally low in fat, especially if you remove the skin. Most fish is also very lean. Even higher-fat fish such as salmon is as lean or leaner than poultry and lean beef.

- Remove all visible fat on poultry before cooking. Most fat is in the skin, making it easier to remove than red meat fat, which tends to be marbled throughout. Although it isn't necessary to remove the poultry skin before cooking, as little fat is absorbed into the meat, it should be removed before eating.

- When buying ground turkey, look for packages labeled as lean turkey or ground breast.

- Fin fish and shellfish are generally lower in fat than meats and poultry. Shellfish are higher than fin fish in cholesterol (shrimp are highest). Imitation seafood sticks have less cholesterol, but more sodium, than real crabmeat.

- Select lean cuts of meat and trim off all visible fat before cooking. Many leaner cuts of beef, pork and lamb are now available. Trim visible fat before cooking. (It's probably not a good idea to completely eliminate meats from the diet because they are important sources of many nutrients, among them iron and vitamin $B_{12}$, that may be hard to get from other foods.) When buying ground beef, choose extra-lean.

- Rib cuts of beef, pork, veal and lamb are fatty; loin cuts are leaner. Beef and veal flank and round cuts are relatively lean; leg and shoulder cuts should be examined for leanness before buying.

- Choose low-fat or fat-free versions of products, when available.

- Choose water-packed or juice-packed canned foods, when available.

- Baste meats with their own juices or broth rather than added fats.

- Refrigerate canned or homemade chicken broth so the fat will harden on top of the broth; remove fat before using. Or, purchase canned fat-free chicken broth.

- Some dishes traditionally made with several eggs can be successfully made with fat-free, cholesterol-free egg product, all egg whites or only 1 or 2 whole eggs plus several egg whites.

- Double the amount of vegetables, fruits, rice and pasta eaten with meals and reduce the amount of meat.

- Choose meatless meals at least twice each week. Limiting the amount of meat, fish and poultry you eat can help reduce fat, particularly saturated fat, and increase fiber and complex carbohydrates when dried beans and peas, grains, vegetables and fruits are substituted.

- For easier cleanup, line cookie sheets with foil before placing a rack on them—baked-on cooking spray can be difficult to remove from pans.

# A WORD ON SODIUM

The recipes in this book were not developed to be low-sodium but we added only enough salt to give them acceptable flavor. You can do the same thing with your own Chinese recipes. Do not add salt if the recipe uses other ingredients, such as soy sauce, that contain sodium. We call for fat-free, reduced-sodium chicken broth in our recipes because it is the only fat-free chicken broth we have found readily available. It was, therefore, necessary to add a small amount of salt to several recipes to achieve the flavor level we desired. Feel free to adjust the salt level to your own liking.

# FAT BUSTER

The recipes in this book were developed to be lower in fat than traditional Chinese recipes. The great majority of recipes have less than 8 grams of fat per serving, with none higher than 12 grams per serving. The Food and Drug Administration (FDA) developed claims guidelines so that any packaged food product that bears a claim, such as "low in fat," meets the same criteria. This way comparisons between similar products can be made easily. The recipes in this book that have 3 grams of fat or less per serving meet that low-fat criteria and are flagged with an added heart symbol.

# 1

# APPETIZERS

*Sesame Chicken Nuggets (page 14), Stuffed Chinese Mushrooms (page 21), Stuffed Pearl Balls (page 20), Hot Mustard Sauce (page 123), Sweet-and-Sour Plum Sauce (page 122)*

# ❤ SESAME CHICKEN NUGGETS

**10** SERVINGS (4 NUGGETS EACH)

*(photograph on page 13)*

**1 pound boneless, skinless chicken breast halves**

**36 sesame rice crackers**

**2 teaspoons ground ginger**

**1 teaspoon garlic powder**

**1 teaspoon sugar**

**1/4 teaspoon ground red pepper (cayenne)**

**2 tablespoons sesame seed**

**2 egg whites**

**1 teaspoon soy sauce**

Cut chicken into 40 pieces, about 1 1/2 × 1/2 inch each.

Place crackers, ginger, garlic powder, sugar and red pepper in plastic bag with zipper top; seal. Crush mixture finely with rolling pin. Pour crumb mixture into shallow dish; stir in sesame seed. Beat egg whites and soy sauce in small bowl.

Heat oven to 400°. Place wire rack on cookie sheet; lightly spray rack with nonstick cooking spray. Roll each chicken piece in crumb mixture until lightly coated; dip in egg white mixture, then roll again in crumb mixture. Place on rack. Bake 10 to 12 minutes or until chicken is no longer pink in center and crumbs are light golden brown. Serve with sauces for dipping.

| **4 Nuggets:** | | **% Daily Value:** | |
|---|---|---|---|
| Calories | 120 | Vitamin A | 0% |
| Calories from fat | 25 | Vitamin C | 0% |
| Fat, g | 3 | Calcium | 2% |
| Saturated, g | 1 | Iron | 4% |
| Cholesterol, mg | 25 | **Diet Exchanges:** | |
| Sodium, mg | 150 | Starch/bread | 1/2 |
| Carbohydrate, g | 11 | Lean meat | 2 |
| Dietary Fiber, g | 0 | | |
| Protein, g | 12 | | |

# ❤ BARBECUED PORK

**12** SERVINGS

**1/2 cup ketchup**

**1/4 cup hoisin sauce**

**2 tablespoons sugar**

**1 tablespoon dry sherry or white wine, if desired**

**2 teaspoons salt**

**2 cloves garlic, finely chopped**

**1 1/2 pounds pork tenderloin**

**Chinese hot mustard and/or duck (plum) sauce, if desired**

Mix all ingredients except pork and mustard in large glass or plastic bowl. Place pork in bowl; turn to coat. Cover and refrigerate at least 1 hour but no longer than 24 hours.

Heat oven to 450°. Spray rack with nonstick cooking spray in shallow roasting pan. Remove pork from marinade; discard marinade. Place pork on rack in pan. Bake uncovered 30 minutes, turning once, until medium doneness (160°) or slightly pink in center. Cool; cut pork diagonally into 1/4-inch pieces. Serve warm or cold with hot mustard and/or duck sauce.

| **1 Serving:** | | **% Daily Value:** | |
|---|---|---|---|
| Calories | 95 | Vitamin A | 2% |
| Calories from fat | 20 | Vitamin C | 3% |
| Fat, g | 2 | Calcium | 0% |
| Saturated, g | 1 | Iron | 4% |
| Cholesterol, mg | 35 | **Diet Exchanges:** | |
| Sodium, mg | 500 | Lean meat | 1 |
| Carbohydrate, g | 7 | Vegetable | 1 |
| Dietary Fiber, g | 0 | | |
| Protein, g | 12 | | |

# ♥ STEAMED VEGETABLE DUMPLINGS

### 10 SERVINGS (3 DUMPLINGS EACH)

*Don't bother chopping the cabbage—instead, take advantage of preshredded coleslaw mix. It stir-fries beautifully and slashes the preparation time for the filling.*

**Horseradish Dipping Sauce (page 121)**

**6 dried black (shiitake) mushrooms**

**4 cups coleslaw mix (8 ounces)**

**1/3 cup chopped green onions (4 medium)**

**1 teaspoon grated gingerroot**

**2 cloves garlic, finely chopped**

**2 tablespoons soy sauce**

**1/2 teaspoon sesame oil**

**30 wonton or siu mai skins**

Prepare Horseradish Dipping Sauce. Soak mushrooms in hot water about 20 minutes or until soft; drain. Rinse with warm water; drain. Squeeze out excess moisture. Remove and discard stems; chop caps.

Spray nonstick wok or 12-inch skillet with nonstick cooking spray; heat over medium-high heat until cooking spray starts to bubble. Add mushrooms, coleslaw mix, green onions, gingerroot and garlic; stir-fry about 4 minutes or until vegetables are very tender. Stir in soy sauce and sesame oil; cool.

Brush edges of 1 wonton skin with water. Place 1 scant tablespoon vegetable mixture on center of skin. (Cover remaining skins with plastic wrap to keep them pliable.) Fold bottom corner of wonton skin over filling to opposite corner, forming a triangle; pleat unfolded edges. (Cover filled dumplings with plastic wrap to keep them from drying out.) Repeat with remaining skins and vegetable mixture.

Place dumplings on heatproof plate; place plate on rack in steamer. Cover and steam over boiling water in wok or Dutch oven 15 minutes. Serve hot with dipping sauce.

| 3 Dumplings: | | % Daily Value: | |
|---|---|---|---|
| Calories | 110 | Vitamin A | 20% |
| Calories from fat | 10 | Vitamin C | 6% |
| Fat, g | 1 | Calcium | 6% |
| Saturated, g | 0 | Iron | 8% |
| Cholesterol, mg | 0 | **Diet Exchanges:** | |
| Sodium, mg | 780 | Starch | 1 |
| Carbohydrate, g | 22 | Vegetable | 1 |
| Dietary Fiber, g | 1 | | |
| Protein, g | 4 | | |

# ♥ CURRIED TURNOVERS

### 24 SERVINGS (3 TURNOVERS EACH)

*By using cooking spray instead of butter, phyllo dough can still be used for crisp appetizers or delicate desserts—the dough itself is fat-free. These spicy turnovers can be made ahead; wrap and freeze, and bake when you like. Increase baking time to 18 to 22 minutes.*

**Cilantro Dipping Sauce (page 120), if desired**

**1/2 pound ground chicken**

**2 teaspoons soy sauce**

**1 cup thinly sliced leek**

**1 1/2 teaspoons curry powder**

**2/3 cup mashed cooked potato**

**2 tablespoons dry sherry or fat-free reduced-sodium chicken**

**1 package (16 ounces) frozen phyllo sheets (18 × 14 inches), thawed**

Prepare Cilantro Dipping Sauce. Spray nonstick wok or 12-inch skillet with nonstick cooking spray; heat over medium-high heat until cooking spray starts to bubble. Add chicken; stir-fry until longer pink. Remove chicken from wok; drain. Mix chicken and soy sauce.

Cool wok slightly. Wipe wok clean, respray with cooking spray and heat over medium-high heat until cooking spray starts to bubble. Add leek; stir-fry 2 to 3 minutes or until tender (add a small amount of water if necessary to prevent sticking). Stir in curry powder; cook about 30 seconds or until fragrant. Stir in chicken, potato and sherry.

Heat oven to 375°. Spray cookie sheet with cooking spray. Place 1 phyllo sheet on work surface; spray lightly with cooking spray. Top with another phyllo sheet; spray with cooking spray. (Cover remaining phyllo sheets with waxed paper, then damp towel to prevent them from drying out). Cut sprayed phyllo crosswise into 5 strips with sharp knife.

Place 1 teaspoon chicken mixture on phyllo strip, about 1 inch from end of strip. Fold a corner across the filling and then continue to fold (like a flag) until the strip is all folded. Place on cookie sheet; spray lightly with cooking spray. Repeat with remaining phyllo and chicken mixture. Bake 15 to 17 minutes or until deep golden brown. Serve hot with dipping sauce.

| 3 Turnovers: | | % Daily Value: | |
| --- | --- | --- | --- |
| Calories | 75 | Vitamin A | 0% |
| Calories from fat | 10 | Vitamin C | 0% |
| Fat, g | 1 | Calcium | 0% |
| Saturated, g | 0 | Iron | 4% |
| Cholesterol, mg | 5 | **Diet Exchanges:** | |
| Sodium, mg | 110 | Starch/bread | 1 |
| Carbohydrate, g | 14 | | |
| Dietary Fiber, g | 0 | | |
| Protein, g | 3 | | |

# ♥ EGG ROLLS

ABOUT **12** EGG ROLLS

*Baking, instead of deep-fat frying, makes many favorite Chinese appetizers into low-fat treats. Still crunchy on the outside, these delicious egg rolls have a fraction of the fat of the originals.*

**Hot-Sweet Apricot Mustard (page 123)**

**8 medium dried black (shiitake) mushrooms**

**4 cups finely shredded green cabbage**

**1 cup bean sprouts (2 ounces)**

**1/3 cup chopped green onions (4 medium)**

**1/2 pound cooked shrimp, finely chopped**

**3/4 teaspoon five-spice powder**

**1/4 teaspoon salt**

**1 tablespoon soy sauce**

**1 1/2 teaspoons grated gingerroot**

**1/2 pound egg roll skins**

**1 egg, beaten**

Prepare Hot-Sweet Apricot Mustard. Soak mushrooms in hot water about 20 minutes or until soft; drain. Rinse with warm water; drain. Squeeze out excess moisture. Remove and discard stems; cut caps into thin strips.

Heat oven to 400°. Spray nonstick wok or 12-inch skillet with nonstick cooking spray; heat over medium-high heat until cooking spray starts to bubble. Add cabbage and bean sprouts; stir-fry 2 minutes. Add green onions; stir-fry 2 minutes (add 1 tablespoon water if necessary to prevent sticking). Stir in shrimp, mushrooms, five-spice powder, salt, soy sauce and gingerroot.

Place wire rack on cookie sheet; spray rack with nonstick cooking spray. Place 1/4 cup cabbage mixture slightly below center on 1 egg roll skin. (Cover remaining skins with plastic wrap to keep them pliable.) Fold corner of egg roll skin closest to filling over filling, tucking the point under. Fold in

and overlap the 2 opposite corners. Brush fourth corner with egg; roll up to seal. Repeat with remaining egg roll skins. (Cover filled egg rolls with plastic wrap to keep them from drying out.)

Place egg rolls, seam sides down, on rack on cookie sheet. Spray lightly with cooking spray. Bake 15 to 20 minutes, turning once, until golden brown. Serve with apricot mustard.

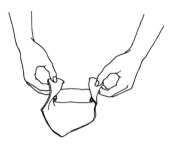

*1. Fold corner over filling; tuck point under filling.*

*2. Fold in and overlap the two opposite corners. Brush remaining corner with egg; roll up to seal.*

| 1 Egg Roll: | | % Daily Value: | |
| --- | --- | --- | --- |
| Calories | 115 | Vitamin A | 2% |
| Calories from fat | 10 | Vitamin C | 8% |
| Fat, g | 1 | Calcium | 4% |
|   Saturated, g | 0 | Iron | 10% |
| Cholesterol, mg | 55 | **Diet Exchanges:** | |
| Sodium, mg | 310 | Starch/bread | 1 |
| Carbohydrate, g | 21 | Vegetable | 1 |
|   Dietary Fiber, g | 2 | | |
| Protein, g | 7 | | |

# ♥ CHILLED SPRING ROLLS

## 10 SPRING ROLLS

**2 green onions**

**5 cups bean sprouts (10 ounces)**

**10 cooked fresh crab legs, shelled, or imitation whole crab legs (each about 2 inches long)**

**1 teaspoon sesame oil**

**10 leaf lettuce leaves**

**10 (8 1/2-inch square) ready-to-eat spring roll skins**

**1/3 cup chopped fresh cilantro**

**Honey Sichuan Sauce (page 123)**

Cut green onions into 2-inch pieces; cut pieces lengthwise into thin strips. Mix green onions and bean sprouts; divide mixture into 10 equal parts. Sprinkle crabmeat pieces with sesame oil. Tear each lettuce leaf into 3-inch square.

Place 1 lettuce square on center of 1 spring roll skin. (Cover remaining skins with plastic wrap to keep them pliable.) Place 1 part bean sprout mixture on lettuce; top with 1 crabmeat piece and 1 1/2 teaspoons cilantro. Fold bottom corner of spring roll skin over filling, tucking the point under. Fold in and overlap the 2 opposite corners. Brush fourth corner generously with cold water; roll up to seal. Repeat with remaining spring roll skins. (Cover filled spring rolls with plastic wrap to keep them from drying out.) Cover and refrigerate at least 2 hours but no longer than 8 hours. Cut in half if desired. Serve with Honey Sichuan Sauce.

| 1 Spring Roll: | | % Daily Value: | |
|---|---|---|---|
| Calories | 130 | Vitamin A | 0% |
| Calories from fat | 25 | Vitamin C | 12% |
| Fat, g | 3 | Calcium | 6% |
| Saturated, g | 0 | Iron | 6% |
| Cholesterol, mg | 45 | **Diet Exchanges:** | |
| Sodium, mg | 220 | Starch/bread | 1 |
| Carbohydrate, g | 15 | Lean meat | 1 |
| Dietary Fiber, g | 1 | | |
| Protein, g | 12 | | |

# ♥ COLD GINGER-SESAME NOODLES

## 8 SERVINGS

**1 package (8 ounces) dried thin Chinese noodles or uncooked angel hair pasta**

**1/4 cup fat-free reduced-sodium chicken broth**

**2 tablespoons thinly sliced green onions**

**1 1/2 tablespoons grated gingerroot**

**1 tablespoon Chinese black vinegar or balsamic vinegar**

**1 tablespoon soy sauce**

**1 tablespoon sesame oil**

**1 teaspoon sugar**

**1 1/2 teaspoons chile puree with garlic**

**1 tablespoon toasted sesame seed**

**Chopped fresh cilantro**

Cook noodles as directed on package just until tender; drain well. Mix broth, green onions, gingerroot, vinegar, soy sauce, sesame oil, sugar and chile puree in large bowl. Add noodles; toss.

Cover and refrigerate 4 to 6 hours to blend flavors. Stir in sesame seed and cilantro before serving.

| 1 Serving: | | % Daily Value: | |
|---|---|---|---|
| Calories | 85 | Vitamin A | 0% |
| Calories from fat | 20 | Vitamin C | 0% |
| Fat, g | 2 | Calcium | 0% |
| Saturated, g | 0 | Iron | 2% |
| Cholesterol, mg | 0 | **Diet Exchanges:** | |
| Sodium, mg | 150 | Starch/bread | 1 |
| Carbohydrate, g | 16 | | |
| Dietary Fiber, g | 0 | | |
| Protein, g | 1 | | |

*Chilled Spring Rolls with Honey Sichuan Sauce*

# ♥ STUFFED PEARL BALLS

## 10 SERVINGS (3 MEATBALLS EACH)

*(photograph on page 13)*

*Glutinous rice, also known as sweet or sticky rice, gets its sticky character from a high starch content. While you want to avoid sticky rice as a side dish, here it's the perfect "pearl" coating for these hearty tidbits.*

**3/4 cup uncooked glutinous or medium-grain rice**

**Lime-Mustard Sauce (page 123)**

**1 pound extra-lean ground turkey breast**

**2 tablespoons soy sauce**

**1 tablespoon oyster sauce**

**2 teaspoons dry sherry, if desired**

**1/2 teaspoon sugar**

**1/2 teaspoon sesame oil**

**3/4 cup frozen (thawed) chopped spinach, squeezed to drain**

**1 tablespoon soy sauce**

**1/2 teaspoon sesame oil**

**1/4 teaspoon ground ginger**

**Duck (plum) sauce, if desired**

Cover rice with cold water in small bowl; let stand 1 hour. Drain rice well; spread on plate. Prepare Lime-Mustard Sauce.

Mix turkey, 2 tablespoons soy sauce, the oyster sauce, sherry, sugar and 1/2 teaspoon sesame oil. Mix spinach, 1 tablespoon soy sauce, 1/2 teaspoon sesame oil and the ginger.

Wet hands with water; place 1 tablespoon turkey mixture in palm of hand and flatten into a small patty. Place about 1 teaspoon spinach mixture in center; fold turkey over spinach mixture and roll lightly into 1 1/2-inch ball. Roll meatball in rice until coated. Repeat with remaining turkey and spinach mixtures, keeping hands wet so mixture does not stick. (Meatballs can be prepared ahead, then covered and refrigerated up to 4 hours; let stand 15 minutes at room temperature before steaming.)

Place meatballs on heatproof plate; place plate on rack in steamer. Cover and steam over boiling water in wok or Dutch oven 20 to 25 minutes or until turkey is no longer pink and rice is tender. Serve hot with mustard sauce and duck sauce.

| 3 Meatballs: | | % Daily Value: | |
|---|---|---|---|
| Calories | 125 | Vitamin A | 6% |
| Calories from fat | 20 | Vitamin C | 0% |
| Fat, g | 2 | Calcium | 2% |
| Saturated, g | 1 | Iron | 6% |
| Cholesterol, mg | 25 | **Diet Exchanges:** | |
| Sodium, mg | 480 | Starch/bread | 1 |
| Carbohydrate, g | 14 | Lean meat | 1 |
| Dietary Fiber, g | 0 | | |
| Protein, g | 13 | | |

# ♥ STUFFED CHINESE MUSHROOMS

**8** SERVINGS (3 MUSHROOMS EACH)

*(photograph on page 13)*

*Hoisin Dipping Sauce (page 120) makes a good dip for these delicious mushrooms. Broiling, rather than baking, really cuts the cooking time on these stuffed mushrooms.*

**24 large mushrooms**

**1/3 cup chopped onion**

**1 teaspoon grated gingerroot**

**4 cloves garlic, finely chopped**

**3 tablespoons dry sherry or fat-free reduced-sodium chicken broth**

**1/4 pound cooked small shrimp, finely chopped**

**6 canned whole water chestnuts, finely chopped**

**1/4 cup finely chopped turkey ham**

**1/4 cup dry bread crumbs**

**1 tablespoon chopped fresh parsley**

**1/4 teaspoon sesame oil**

Set oven control to broil. Remove stems from mushroom caps; set stems aside. Place mushroom caps, stem sides down, in ungreased jelly roll pan, 15 1/2 × 10 1/2 × 1 inch. Broil with tops about 4 inches from heat about 8 minutes or until mushrooms begin to release moisture. Remove mushrooms from pan; drain on paper towels. Finely chop mushroom stems.

Spray nonstick wok or 12-inch skillet with nonstick cooking spray; heat over medium-high heat until cooking spray starts to bubble. Add onion, gingerroot, garlic and sherry. Cook about 6 minutes, stirring frequently, until onion is tender. Stir in chopped mushroom stems and remaining ingredients. Heat through.

Place mushroom caps, stem sides up, in ungreased jelly roll pan. Spoon shrimp mixture into caps, mounding slightly. Spray lightly with cooking spray. Broil with tops 4 inches from heat about 5 minutes or until shrimp mixture is light brown.

| 3 Mushrooms: | | % Daily Value: | |
|---|---|---|---|
| Calories | 60 | Vitamin A | 0% |
| Calories from fat | 10 | Vitamin C | 4% |
| Fat, g | 1 | Calcium | 2% |
| Saturated, g | 0 | Iron | 8% |
| Cholesterol, mg | 30 | **Diet Exchanges:** | |
| Sodium, mg | 100 | Vegetable | 2 |
| Carbohydrate, g | 8 | | |
| Dietary Fiber, g | 1 | | |
| Protein, g | 6 | | |

# ♥ SICHUAN EGGPLANT SPREAD

## ABOUT 2 CUPS SPREAD

*Look for smaller eggplants as they generally have fewer seeds and a smoother flavor. Roasting the garlic gives it a milder, sweeter taste that blends well with the other seasonings. It's good on low-fat crackers.*

**2 small eggplant (2 pounds)**
**6 large cloves garlic, unpeeled**
**1 tablespoon grated gingerroot**
**1 tablespoon lemon juice**
**1 tablespoon soy sauce**
**3/4 teaspoon ground coriander**
**3/4 teaspoon sesame oil**
**1/4 teaspoon fennel seed, crushed**
**1/4 teaspoon ground red pepper (cayenne)**

Heat oven to 400°. Spray cookie sheet with nonstick cooking spray. Place eggplant on cookie sheet; pierce several times with fork. Wrap garlic in aluminum foil; place on cookie sheet with eggplant. Bake about 30 minutes or until garlic is tender; remove garlic from oven. Continue baking eggplant about 45 minutes longer or until blackened and collapsed. Let stand until cool enough to handle.

Cut eggplant in half. Scrape out pulp onto chopping board; discard skin. Squeeze roasted garlic out of skins onto eggplant. Coarsely chop eggplant with garlic; place in medium glass or plastic bowl. Stir in remaining ingredients until well blended. Serve at room temperature, or cover and refrigerate until chilled.

| 2 Tablespoons: | | % Daily Value: | |
|---|---|---|---|
| Calories | 10 | Vitamin A | 0% |
| Calories from fat | 0 | Vitamin C | 0% |
| Fat, g | 0 | Calcium | 0% |
| Saturated, g | 0 | Iron | 0% |
| Cholesterol, mg | 0 | **Diet Exchanges:** | |
| Sodium, mg | 100 | Free food | |
| Carbohydrate, g | 4 | | |
| Dietary Fiber, g | 1 | | |
| Protein, g | 0 | | |

# ♥ SHRIMP TOAST

## 10 SERVINGS (2 TOASTS EACH)

*Baking these toasts on a rack allows the hot air in the oven to circulate around them, so they are crispy, without fat-laden deep frying!*

**1/2 pound uncooked shrimp, peeled, deveined and coarsely chopped**
**1/2 cup chopped green onions (5 medium)**
**1/4 cup all-purpose flour**
**1/4 cup water**
**1 tablespoon cornstarch**
**1/2 teaspoon salt**
**1/2 teaspoon sesame oil**
**1/4 teaspoon sugar**
**Dash of white pepper**
**2 egg whites**
**1 baguette (8 ounces), cut into 3/8-inch diagonal slices**

Heat oven to 425°. Place wire rack on cookie sheet; spray rack with nonstick cooking spray. Mix all ingredients except bread.

Spread about 1 tablespoon shrimp mixture on each bread slice. Place slices on rack on cookie sheet. Spray lightly with cooking spray. Bake about 15 minutes or until edges of bread are deep golden brown and crisp.

| 2 Toasts: | | % Daily Value: | |
|---|---|---|---|
| Calories | 85 | Vitamin A | 0% |
| Calories from fat | 10 | Vitamin C | 0% |
| Fat, g | 1 | Calcium | 2% |
| Saturated, g | 0 | Iron | 6% |
| Cholesterol, mg | 20 | **Diet Exchanges:** | |
| Sodium, mg | 280 | Starch/bread | 1 |
| Carbohydrate, g | 15 | | |
| Dietary Fiber, g | 1 | | |
| Protein, g | 5 | | |

*Shrimp Toast*

# ♥ CHINESE CHICKEN SALAD WITH PEANUT DRESSING

### 4 SERVINGS

*Leftover egg roll skins can be used to make the crispy wonton strips. They are also great for low-fat snacking!*

**Crispy Wonton Strips (right)**

**Warm Peanut Dressing (page 126)**

**1 can (8 ounces) pineapple tidbits in juice, drained and juice reserved**

**1/2 pound Chinese pea pods (2 cups)**

**6 cups shredded romaine**

**1 large red bell pepper, cut lengthwise into fourths and sliced crosswise**

**1 cup shredded cooked chicken breast**

**1/4 cup sliced green onions (3 medium)**

Prepare Crispy Wonton Strips and Warm Peanut Dressing, using reserved pineapple juice for the dressing recipe.

Remove strings from pea pods. Place pea pods in boiling water. Cover and cook 1 minute; drain. Immediately rinse with cold water; drain. Cut pea pods in half.

Toss romaine, pea pods, bell pepper and pineapple. Divide among 4 plates. Top with chicken, peanut dressing and green onions. Garnish with wonton strips.

CRISPY WONTON STRIPS

**1 tablespoon water**

**1 tablespoon soy sauce**

**Dash of garlic powder**

**12 wonton skins**

**Sesame seed, if desired**

Heat oven to 350°. Spray cookie sheet with non-stick cooking spray. Mix water, soy sauce and garlic powder; brush on wonton skins. Cut each skin into 3/8-inch strips. Place strips on cookie sheet. Sprinkle with sesame seed. Bake 6 to 8 minutes or until golden brown; cool.

| 1 Serving: | | % Daily Value: | |
|---|---|---|---|
| Calories | 285 | Vitamin A | 28% |
| Calories from fat | 65 | Vitamin C | 100% |
| Fat, g | 7 | Calcium | 12% |
| Saturated, g | 1 | Iron | 22% |
| Cholesterol, mg | 25 | **Diet Exchanges:** | |
| Sodium, mg | 650 | Starch/bread | 1 |
| Carbohydrate, g | 39 | Lean meat | 2 |
| Dietary Fiber, g | 4 | Vegetable | 2 |
| Protein, g | 20 | Fruit | 1 |

*Chinese Chicken Salad with Warm Peanut Dressing, Hot-and-Sour Cucumber and Jicama (page 27)*

# ❤ DUCK FRUIT SALAD

### 4 SERVINGS

**3/4 cup Sweet-Hot Plum Sauce (page 122)**

**1 head Boston lettuce**

**1 ripe papaya or 1/2 cantaloupe or honey-dew melon, sliced**

**1 Asian or Bostic pear, sliced**

**1 can (11 ounces) mandarin orange segments, drained**

**1/2 pound roasted duck breast or cooked turkey tenderloin, sliced**

**2 green onions, sliced**

**Toasted cashews**

Prepare Sweet-Hot Plum Sauce. Arrange lettuce leaves on 4 dinner plates. Arrange papaya and pear slices on lettuce. Top with orange segments and sliced duck. Spoon plum sauce over each salad. Top with green onions and cashews.

| 1 Serving: | | % Daily Value: | |
|---|---|---|---|
| Calories | 370 | Vitamin A | 4% |
| Calories from fat | 65 | Vitamin C | 100% |
| Fat, g | 7 | Calcium | 6% |
| Saturated, g | 3 | Iron | 14% |
| Cholesterol, mg | 50 | **Diet Exchanges:** | |
| Sodium, mg | 120 | Lean meat | 2 |
| Carbohydrate, g | 65 | Vegetable | 1 |
| Dietary Fiber, g | 5 | Fruit | 4 |
| Protein, g | 17 | | |

# ❤ SWEET-AND-SOUR SPINACH SALAD

### 6 SERVINGS

*The deliciously spicy dressing would be equally good on a fruit salad.*

**Sweet-and-Sour Dressing (below)**

**8 cups bite-size pieces spinach leaves**

**1 large red or yellow bell pepper, cut lengthwise in half and sliced crosswise**

**1 can (8 ounces) sliced water chestnuts, drained**

**4 ounces sliced button mushrooms or 4 ounces enoki mushrooms, separated**

**Pine nuts, toasted, if desired**

Prepare Sweet-and-Sour Dressing. Mix spinach, bell pepper, water chestnuts and mushrooms in large salad bowl. Pour dressing over salad; toss. Garnish with pine nuts.

### SWEET-AND-SOUR DRESSING

**1/4 cup duck (plum) sauce**

**3 tablespoons red wine vinegar**

**2 tablespoons hoisin sauce**

**1 teaspoon grated orange peel**

**1 teaspoon vegetable oil**

**1 teaspoon chile puree with garlic**

Mix all ingredients.

| 1 Serving: | | % Daily Value: | |
|---|---|---|---|
| Calories | 80 | Vitamin A | 74% |
| Calories from fat | 10 | Vitamin C | 100% |
| Fat, g | 1 | Calcium | 8% |
| Saturated, g | 0 | Iron | 16% |
| Cholesterol, mg | 0 | **Diet Exchanges:** | |
| Sodium, mg | 190 | Vegetable | 1 |
| Carbohydrate, g | 18 | Fruit | 1 |
| Dietary Fiber, g | 3 | | |
| Protein, g | 3 | | |

# ♥ HOT-AND-SOUR CUCUMBER AND JICAMA

**4** SERVINGS

*(photograph on page 25)*

*Crisp and sweet-tart, this do-ahead salad would be great paired with Red-Cooked Sea Bass (page 57).*

**1 long slender cucumber (10 ounces)**

**1 small jicama (3/4 pound)**

**1 clove garlic, finely chopped**

**2 tablespoons sugar**

**1/4 teaspoon salt**

**1/4 teaspoon crushed red pepper**

**2 tablespoons rice vinegar**

**Chopped fresh cilantro, if desired**

Cut cucumber lengthwise in half; remove seeds. Cut each half lengthwise into 4 strips; cut strips crosswise into 1/2-inch pieces. Peel jicama; cut into 1/2-inch cubes.

Spray nonstick wok or 12-inch skillet with nonstick cooking spray; heat over medium-high heat until cooking spray starts to bubble. Add cucumber, jicama and garlic; stir-fry 2 to 3 minutes or just until cucumber skin is bright green. Stir in sugar, salt and red pepper.

Spoon into medium glass or plastic bowl. Cover and refrigerate about 2 hours or until chilled. Stir in vinegar just before serving. Garnish with cilantro.

| 1 Serving: | | % Daily Value: | |
|---|---|---|---|
| Calories | 60 | Vitamin A | 2% |
| Calories from fat | 0 | Vitamin C | 16% |
| Fat, g | 0 | Calcium | 2% |
| Saturated, g | 0 | Iron | 4% |
| Cholesterol, mg | 0 | **Diet Exchanges:** | |
| Sodium, mg | 140 | Vegetable | 3 |
| Carbohydrate, g | 16 | | |
| Dietary Fiber, g | 2 | | |
| Protein, g | 1 | | |

# ♥ SPINACH EGG DROP SOUP

**6** SERVINGS

**5 cups fat-free reduced-sodium chicken broth**

**3 thin slices gingerroot, 1 × 1/8-inch**

**3 cups sliced spinach (2 ounces)**

**4 ounces firm lite tofu, cut into 1/2-inch cubes**

**1 egg***

**2 egg whites***

**1 tablespoon dry sherry, if desired**

**1/4 teaspoon salt**

**Dash of white pepper**

Heat broth and gingerroot to boiling in 3-quart saucepan; reduce heat. Stir in spinach and tofu. Simmer uncovered about 3 minutes or until spinach is wilted. Remove gingerroot.

Beat egg, egg whites and sherry salt and white pepper until foamy. Heat broth mixture to boiling. Pour egg mixture slowly into broth mixture, stirring constantly with fork until egg mixture forms threads. Immediately remove from heat.

*1/2 cup fat-free cholesterol-free egg product can be substituted for the 1 egg and 2 egg whites.

| 1 Serving: | | % Daily Value: | |
|---|---|---|---|
| Calories | 45 | Vitamin A | 24% |
| Calories from fat | 10 | Vitamin C | 6% |
| Fat, g | 1 | Calcium | 8% |
| Saturated, g | 0 | Iron | 16% |
| Cholesterol, mg | 35 | **Diet Exchanges:** | |
| Sodium, mg | 500 | Lean meat | 1 |
| Carbohydrate, g | 3 | | |
| Dietary Fiber, g | 1 | | |
| Protein, g | 7 | | |

# ♥ HOT-AND-SOUR SOUP

## 6 SERVINGS

**6 medium dried black (shiitake) mushrooms**

**1/2 package (10.5-ounce size) firm lite tofu**

**4 cups fat-free reduced-sodium chicken broth**

**1/4 cup rice or white vinegar**

**1 tablespoon soy sauce**

**1/2 teaspoon salt**

**1/2 cup canned sliced bamboo shoots, cut into thin julienne strips**

**1 medium carrot, cut into thin julienne strips (1 1/2 inches long)**

**1 1/2 tablespoons chopped pimiento**

**2 tablespoons cornstarch**

**2 tablespoons cold water**

**1/4 teaspoon white pepper**

**2 egg whites or 1/4 cup fat-free cholesterol-free egg product**

**2 tablespoons chopped green onions**

**2 teaspoons red pepper sauce**

**1/2 teaspoon sesame oil**

Soak mushrooms in hot water about 20 minutes or until soft; drain. Rinse with warm water; drain. Squeeze out excess moisture. Remove and discard stems; cut caps into thin slices. Cut tofu into 1 1/2 × 1/4-inch pieces.

Heat broth, vinegar, soy sauce and salt to boiling in 3-quart saucepan. Stir in mushrooms, bamboo shoots and carrot. Heat to boiling; reduce heat. Cover and simmer about 10 minutes or until carrot is tender. Stir in tofu and pimiento.

Mix 2 tablespoons cornstarch, the cold water and white pepper; stir into broth mixture. Heat to rolling boil, stirring constantly. Beat egg whites until foamy; pour slowly into broth mixture, stirring constantly with fork until egg whites form threads. Stir in green onions, pepper sauce and sesame oil.

| 1 Serving: | | % Daily Value: | |
|---|---|---|---|
| Calories | 55 | Vitamin A | 20% |
| Calories from fat | 10 | Vitamin C | 4% |
| Fat, g | 1 | Calcium | 4% |
| Saturated, g | 0 | Iron | 14% |
| Cholesterol, mg | 0 | **Diet Exchanges:** | |
| Sodium, mg | 680 | Lean meat | 1/2 |
| Carbohydrate, g | 7 | Vegetable | 1 |
| Dietary Fiber, g | 1 | | |
| Protein, g | 6 | | |

# ♥ WONTON SOUP

**8** SERVINGS

**1/4 pound uncooked shrimp, peeled, deveined and finely chopped**

**2 ounces lean ground turkey**

**3 canned whole water chestnuts, finely chopped**

**2 green onions, finely chopped**

**1 teaspoon cornstarch**

**1/2 teaspoon salt**

**1/4 teaspoon sesame oil**

**Dash of white pepper**

**24 wonton skins (about 1/2 pound)**

**1 egg white, slightly beaten**

**5 cups water**

**1/4 pound Chinese pea pods (1 cup)**

**1/4 pound mushrooms**

**4 cups fat-free reduced-sodium chicken broth**

**1/4 cup canned sliced bamboo shoots**

**1/4 teaspoon salt**

**Dash of white pepper**

**2 tablespoons chopped green onions**

**1/4 teaspoon sesame oil**

Mix shrimp, turkey, water chestnuts, 2 green onions, 1 teaspoon cornstarch, 1/2 teaspoon salt, 1/4 teaspoon sesame oil and dash of white pepper.

Place 1/2 teaspoon shrimp mixture on center of 1 wonton skin. (Cover remaining skins with plastic wrap to keep them pliable.) Fold bottom corner of wonton skin over filling to opposite corner, forming a triangle. Brush right corner of triangle with egg white. Bring corners together below filling; pinch left corner to right corner to seal. Repeat with remaining wonton skins. (Cover filled wontons with plastic wrap to keep them from drying out.)

Heat water to boiling in Dutch oven; add wontons. Heat to boiling; reduce heat. Simmer uncovered 2 minutes; drain. Immediately rinse wontons with cold water; cover with iced water to keep them from sticking together.

Remove strings from pea pods. Place pea pods in boiling water. Cover and cook 1 minute; drain. Immediately rinse with cold water; drain. Cut pea pods lengthwise in half. Cut mushrooms into 1/4-inch slices.

Heat broth and mushrooms to boiling in Dutch oven. Drain wontons. Stir wontons, bamboo shoots, 1/4 teaspoon salt and dash of white pepper into broth mixture. Heat to boiling; reduce heat. Simmer uncovered 2 minutes. Stir in pea pods, 2 tablespoons green onions and 1/4 teaspoon sesame oil.

| 1 Serving: | | % Daily Value: | |
| --- | --- | --- | --- |
| Calories | 110 | Vitamin A | 0% |
| Calories from fat | 10 | Vitamin C | 8% |
| Fat, g | 1 | Calcium | 6% |
| Saturated, g | 0 | Iron | 10% |
| Cholesterol, mg | 10 | **Diet Exchanges:** | |
| Sodium, mg | 580 | Starch/bread | 1 |
| Carbohydrate, g | 19 | Vegetable | 1 |
| Dietary Fiber, g | 1 | | |
| Protein, g | 7 | | |

# ♥ CORN-CRAB EGG DROP SOUP

**6** SERVINGS

*Imitation crabmeat is made from pollack, a mild white fish that is extremely low in fat. An acceptable substitute for real crabmeat, imitation crabmeat is readily available and less expensive. Use it in salads or even stir-fries. Stir additional vinegar into the soup if you like a more sour-tart flavor.*

**3 cups fat-free reduced-sodium chicken broth**

**1 can (15 ounces) cream-style corn**

**1 tablespoon soy sauce**

**1 tablespoon dry sherry, if desired**

**1 teaspoon grated gingerroot**

**1/4 teaspoon salt**

**Dash of white pepper**

**1 tablespoon cornstarch**

**2 tablespoons cold water**

**8 ounces imitation seafood sticks or cooked real king crabmeat, coarsely flaked**

**2 tablespoons sliced green onions**

**2 egg whites or 1/4 cup fat-free cholesterol-free egg product**

**1 teaspoon cider vinegar**

**1/2 teaspoon sesame oil**

**Red pepper sauce to taste, if desired**

**Cider vinegar, if desired**

Mix broth, corn, soy sauce, sherry, gingerroot, salt and white pepper in 3-quart saucepan. Heat to boiling over medium heat, stirring occasionally. Mix cornstarch and cold water. Stir cornstarch mixture, seafood and onions into broth mixture. Cook 1 to 2 minutes or until thickened; remove from heat.

Beat egg whites slightly (not until foamy); pour slowly into broth mixture, stirring constantly with fork until egg whites form threads. Stir in 1 teaspoon vinegar and the sesame oil. Serve with pepper sauce and additional vinegar.

| 1 Serving: | | % Daily Value: | |
|---|---|---|---|
| Calories | 120 | Vitamin A | 2% |
| Calories from fat | 20 | Vitamin C | 4% |
| Fat, g | 2 | Calcium | 0% |
| Saturated, g | 0 | Iron | 4% |
| Cholesterol, mg | 10 | **Diet Exchanges:** | |
| Sodium, mg | 1050 | Starch/bread | 1 |
| Carbohydrate, g | 18 | Lean meat | 1 |
| Dietary Fiber, g | 1 | | |
| Protein, g | 9 | | |

*Corn-Crab Egg Drop Soup*

# 2

# CHICKEN MAIN DISHES

*Spicy Chicken with Cabbage (page 40)*

## BAKED SESAME CHICKEN

### 4 SERVINGS

*Chinese hot mustard holds the sesame seed and rice cracker coating in place in this baked chicken recipe. If you'd like your chicken a little less spicy, dilute the mustard with one tablespoon nonfat mayonnaise. Rice crackers (not cakes) are available plain, unsalted or in spicy mixtures.*

**4 skinless boneless chicken breast halves (about 1 pound)**

**2 to 3 teaspoons purchased Chinese hot mustard or Hot Mustard Sauce (page 123)**

**1 1/2 cups rice crackers, crushed (1 cup)**

**2 teaspoons sesame seed**

**1/4 cup apricot spreadable fruit, melted, if desired**

Heat oven to 425°. Spray rectangular baking dish, 11 × 7 × 1 1/2 inches, with nonstick cooking spray. Spread 1 side of each chicken breast half with mustard. Mix cracker crumbs and sesame seed in plastic bag. Add 1 chicken breast half at a time. Seal bag and shake to coat chicken, covering completely. Place chicken in baking dish. Sprinkle any remaining crumb mixture over chicken.

Spray chicken lightly with cooking spray, about 3 seconds. Bake uncovered 25 to 30 minutes or until juice of chicken is no longer pink when centers of thickest pieces are cut. Drizzle with melted fruit spread.

| 1 Serving: | | % Daily Value: | |
|---|---|---|---|
| Calories | 195 | Vitamin A | 0% |
| Calories from fat | 45 | Vitamin C | 0% |
| Fat, g | 5 | Calcium | 2% |
| Saturated, g | 1 | Iron | 6% |
| Cholesterol, mg | 60 | **Diet Exchanges:** | |
| Sodium, mg | 200 | Starch/bread | 1 |
| Carbohydrate, g | 12 | Lean meat | 2 |
| Dietary Fiber, g | 0 | | |
| Protein, g | 26 | | |

## ♥ BAKED LEMON CHICKEN

### 4 SERVINGS

**4 skinless boneless chicken breast halves (about 1 pound)**

**1 egg white**

**1 teaspoon water**

**1/4 cup all-purpose flour**

**1 teaspoon baking soda**

**1/4 to 1/2 teaspoon ground red pepper (cayenne), if desired**

**Chinese Lemon Sauce (page 121)**

**Chopped green onions and lemon slices**

Cut breasts crosswise in half. Mix egg white and water in medium bowl. Add chicken; turn chicken to coat. Let stand 10 minutes.

Heat oven to 450°. Spray nonstick cookie sheet with nonstick cooking spray. Remove chicken from egg mixture; discard egg mixture. Mix flour, baking soda and red pepper in plastic bag. Add 1 chicken piece at a time. Seal bag and shake to coat chicken. Place chicken on cookie sheet; spray with cooking spray about 5 seconds or until surface of chicken appears moist.

Bake uncovered 20 to 25 minutes or until juice of chicken is no longer pink when centers of thickest pieces are cut. Meanwhile, prepare Chinese Lemon Sauce. Let chicken stand 5 minutes; cut each piece crosswise into about 5 slices. Pour sauce over chicken. Garnish with lemon slices and green onion.

| 1 Serving: | | % Daily Value: | |
|---|---|---|---|
| Calories | 220 | Vitamin A | 0% |
| Calories from fat | 25 | Vitamin C | 2% |
| Fat, g | 3 | Calcium | 2% |
| Saturated, g | 1 | Iron | 8% |
| Cholesterol, mg | 60 | **Diet Exchanges:** | |
| Sodium, mg | 560 | Lean meat | 3 |
| Carbohydrate, g | 22 | Vegetable | 1 |
| Dietary Fiber, g | 0 | Fruit | 1 |
| Protein, g | 26 | | |

*Baked Lemon Chicken*

# ❤ BRAISED CHICKEN IN RED SAUCE

### 8 SERVINGS

*The ancient Chinese technique of cooking chicken in red sauce, a seasoned soy master sauce, is receiving renewed attention because it's flavorful and low in fat. The chicken here is served cut in the Chinese manner, on the bone.*

**2 pounds bone-in chicken breasts (about 2 whole or 4 split breasts with ribs)**

**1/4 cup mushroom soy sauce**

**1/4 cup water**

**2 tablespoons dry white wine or liquid from Pickled Gingerroot (page 127)**

**1 teaspoon sugar**

**1 teaspoon chile puree**

**2 thin slices gingerroot or Pickled Gingerroot (page 127)**

**4 star anise**

**4 Green Onion Flowers (right) or parsley sprigs**

Heat oven to 425°. Spray square pan, 8 × 8 × 2 inches, with nonstick cooking spray. Remove skin from chicken. Place chicken, bone side down, in pan. Cover and bake 25 minutes.

Meanwhile, heat soy sauce, water, wine, sugar, chile puree, gingerroot and star anise to boiling in 1-quart saucepan; reduce heat to low. Simmer uncovered 10 minutes. Remove gingerroot and star anise. Pour sauce over chicken. Bake uncovered 10 to 15 minutes, basting chicken with sauce several times, until juice of chicken is no longer pink when centers of thickest pieces are cut.

Remove chicken from sauce; place sauce in freezer to chill. Cover chicken and let stand 15 minutes. Meanwhile, prepare Green Onion Flowers. Skim fat from chilled sauce; heat sauce to boiling.

Chop chicken into about 2 × 1-inch pieces with Chinese cleaver or large knife. Arrange chicken on serving platter. Garnish with Green Onion Flowers. Serve heated sauce over chicken if desired.

### GREEN ONION FLOWERS

For each flower, remove root and green top from 1 green onion. Cut onion into 3-inch piece. Make 4 crosscuts about 3/4 inch deep on one end; repeat on other end. Place onion in iced water about 10 minutes or until ends curl. Drain and shake off excess water.

| 1 Serving: | | % Daily Value: | |
|---|---|---|---|
| Calories | 100 | Vitamin A | 0% |
| Calories from fat | 20 | Vitamin C | 0% |
| Fat, g | 2 | Calcium | 0% |
| Saturated, g | 1 | Iron | 4% |
| Cholesterol, mg | 45 | **Diet Exchanges:** | |
| Sodium, mg | 560 | Lean meat | 2 |
| Carbohydrate, g | 2 | | |
| Dietary Fiber, g | 0 | | |
| Protein, g | 18 | | |

# SWEET-HOT FUN SEE CHICKEN

### 6 SERVINGS

*We've eliminated deep-frying and added Chinese cabbage for crunch, to give this recipe a new look and a healthier profile.*

**1 pound skinless boneless chicken breast halves**

**1 teaspoon cornstarch**

**1/4 cup water**

**2 tablespoons cornstarch**

**1/2 cup sugar**

**1/2 cup fat-free reduced-sodium chicken broth**

**1/3 cup plus 1 tablespoon seasoned rice vinegar**

**1 teaspoon dark soy sauce**

**1 teaspoon chile puree**

**1 clove garlic, finely chopped**

**4 cups shredded Chinese (napa) cabbage (1/2 pound)**

**2 ounces uncooked cellophane noodles (bean threads) or rice stick noodles, broken into 2-inch pieces**

**1 teaspoon vegetable oil**

**2 tablespoons toasted sesame seed**

Cut chicken into 2 × 1/2-inch strips. Toss chicken and 1 teaspoon cornstarch in medium glass or plastic bowl. Let stand 10 minutes. Mix water and 2 tablespoons cornstarch.

Heat sugar, broth, rice vinegar, soy sauce, chile puree and garlic to boiling in 1-quart saucepan, stirring occasionally. Stir in water-cornstarch mixture. Cook and stir about 1 minute or until thickened; remove from heat and keep warm.

Place cabbage and noodles in large bowl; cover with boiling water. Let stand no more than 5 minutes or until cabbage is crisp-tender and noodles are soft; drain. Place noodle mixture on heated platter.

Spray nonstick wok or 12-inch skillet with nonstick cooking spray; heat over medium-high heat until cooking spray starts to bubble. Add oil; rotate wok to coat side. Add chicken; stir-fry about 3 minutes or until light brown and no longer pink in center. Top noodle mixture with chicken. Heat sauce to boiling; pour over chicken and noodle mixture. Sprinkle with sesame seed.

| 1 Serving: | | % Daily Value: | |
|---|---|---|---|
| Calories | 210 | Vitamin A | 10% |
| Calories from fat | 35 | Vitamin C | 12% |
| Fat, g | 4 | Calcium | 4% |
| Saturated, g | 1 | Iron | 8% |
| Cholesterol, mg | 40 | **Diet Exchanges:** | |
| Sodium, mg | 160 | Starch/bread | 1 |
| Carbohydrate, g | 27 | Lean meat | 2 |
| Dietary Fiber, g | 1 | Vegetable | 2 |
| Protein, g | 18 | | |

# COCONUT CURRY CHICKEN

**4** SERVINGS

*Toasted coconut adds an exotic tropical flavor, but just two tablespoons contain four grams of fat. By limiting the amount of coconut you use and buying reduced-fat coconut milk, you can still enjoy the taste without excess fat and calories.*

**1 tablespoon curry powder**

**3/4 pound skinless boneless chicken breast halves**

**1 teaspoon vegetable oil**

**1 small onion, cut into 2 × 1/4-inch strips**

**1 small zucchini, cut into 1/4-inch slices**

**1 medium green bell pepper, cut into 3/4-inch squares (1 cup)**

**1/3 cup reduced-fat (lite) coconut milk**

**1 tablespoon brown bean sauce**

**1 teaspoon grated gingerroot**

**1/2 teaspoon salt**

**2 tablespoons shredded coconut, toasted**

Rub curry powder on chicken. Cut chicken into 3/4-inch pieces. Let stand 10 minutes. Spray non-stick wok or 12-inch skillet with nonstick cooking spray; heat over medium-high heat until cooking spray starts to bubble. Add chicken; stir-fry 2 minutes. Move chicken to side of wok.

Add oil to center of wok. Add onion, zucchini and bell pepper; stir-fry 2 minutes. Add coconut milk, bean sauce, gingerroot and salt; cook and stir until sauce coats vegetables and chicken and is heated through. Sprinkle with toasted coconut.

| 1 Serving: | | % Daily Value: | |
|---|---|---|---|
| Calories | 155 | Vitamin A | 2% |
| Calories from fat | 55 | Vitamin C | 12% |
| Fat, g | 6 | Calcium | 2% |
| Saturated, g | 3 | Iron | 12% |
| Cholesterol, mg | 45 | **Diet Exchanges:** | |
| Sodium, mg | 350 | Lean meat | 2 |
| Carbohydrate, g | 7 | Vegetable | 1 |
| Dietary Fiber, g | 1 | | |
| Protein, g | 19 | | |

*Coconut Curry Chicken*

# SPICY CHICKEN WITH CABBAGE

**4** SERVINGS

*(photograph on page 33)*

**8 dried black (shiitake) mushrooms**

**3/4 pound skinless boneless chicken thighs**

**1 tablespoon cornstarch**

**1/4 teaspoon salt**

**1/8 teaspoon white pepper**

**2 teaspoons cornstarch**

**1 teaspoon sugar**

**2 teaspoons water**

**1/4 cup fat-free reduced-sodium chicken broth**

**4 cloves garlic, finely chopped**

**2 teaspoons finely chopped gingerroot**

**2 teaspoons chile puree**

**2 teaspoons soy sauce**

**1 teaspoon vegetable oil**

**1/2 medium head green cabbage or Chinese (napa) cabbage, cut into 1-inch pieces (4 cups)**

**4 green onions, cut into 1-inch diagonal pieces**

**1 medium red bell pepper, cut into 1-inch pieces**

Soak mushrooms in hot water about 20 minutes or until soft; drain. Rinse with warm water; drain. Squeeze out excess moisture. Remove and discard stems; cut caps into 1/2-inch pieces.

Cut chicken into 1 × 1/2-inch pieces. Toss chicken, 1 tablespoon cornstarch, the salt and white pepper in medium glass or plastic bowl. Let stand 10 minutes.

Mix 2 teaspoons cornstarch, the sugar and water. Mix broth, garlic, gingerroot, chile puree and soy sauce; stir in cornstarch mixture.

Spray nonstick wok or 12-inch skillet with nonstick cooking spray; heat over medium-high heat until cooking spray starts to bubble. Add oil; rotate wok to coat side. Add chicken; stir-fry 3 to 4 minutes or until chicken is no longer pink in center. Add mushrooms and cabbage; stir-fry 2 minutes.

Stir broth mixture; stir into chicken mixture. Cook and stir 1 to 2 minutes or until thickened. Add green onions and bell pepper; cook and stir 1 to 2 minutes or until chicken mixture is evenly coated.

| 1 Serving: | | % Daily Value: | |
|---|---|---|---|
| Calories | 200 | Vitamin A | 12% |
| Calories from fat | 65 | Vitamin C | 62% |
| Fat, g | 7 | Calcium | 8% |
| Saturated, g | 2 | Iron | 14% |
| Cholesterol, mg | 60 | **Diet Exchanges:** | |
| Sodium, mg | 440 | Starch/bread | 1 |
| Carbohydrate, g | 16 | Lean meat | 2 |
| Dietary Fiber, g | 3 | | |
| Protein, g | 21 | | |

# CHICKEN KUNG PAO

**4** SERVINGS

*Kung Pao Chicken has received negative publicity for being one of the Chinese dishes that's highest in fat. To reduce the fat, we used partially defatted peanuts with half the fat grams, and toasted the nuts in just a light coating of nonstick cooking oil instead of deep-fat frying. Don't worry, this dish still has plenty of nutty crunch!*

1 pound skinless boneless chicken breast halves

1 teaspoon cornstarch

1 tablespoon water

1 egg white

1 tablespoon cornstarch

1 tablespoon cold water

1/2 cup partially defatted roasted peanuts or 1/4 cup dry-roasted peanuts

1 teaspoon sesame oil

2 medium stalks celery, cut into 1/4-inch diagonal slices

1 small leek or onion, cut into 2 × 1/4-inch slices

1 clove garlic, finely chopped

1 teaspoon grated gingerroot

1/2 cup fat-free reduced-sodium chicken broth

1/2 teaspoon sugar

2 tablespoons soy sauce

2 tablespoons hoisin sauce

2 teaspoons chile puree

1 medium green bell pepper, cut into 3/4-inch pieces

Cut chicken into 3/4-inch pieces. Mix 1 teaspoon cornstarch, 1 tablespoon water and the egg white in medium glass or plastic bowl. Stir in chicken. Let stand 10 minutes.

Mix 1 tablespoon cornstarch and 1 tablespoon cold water. Spray nonstick wok or 12-inch skillet with nonstick cooking spray; heat over medium-high heat until cooking spray starts to bubble. Spread peanuts in single layer on paper towel; spray lightly with cooking spray, about 2 seconds. Add to wok; stir-fry about 1 minute or until toasted. Immediately remove from wok; cool.

Add sesame oil to wok; rotate wok to coat side. Add chicken; stir-fry 2 to 3 minutes or until brown and no longer pink in center. Remove chicken from wok. Add celery, leek, garlic and gingerroot to wok; stir-fry 1 minute. Stir in broth, sugar, soy sauce, hoisin sauce and chile puree; heat to boiling. Stir in bell pepper, chicken and cornstarch mixture. Cook and stir about 1 minute or until thickened. Sprinkle with peanuts.

| 1 Serving: | | % Daily Value: | |
|---|---|---|---|
| Calories | 255 | Vitamin A | 4% |
| Calories from fat | 80 | Vitamin C | 22% |
| Fat, g | 9 | Calcium | 4% |
| Saturated, g | 1 | Iron | 10% |
| Cholesterol, mg | 60 | **Diet Exchanges:** | |
| Sodium, mg | 770 | Starch/bread | 1 |
| Carbohydrate, g | 13 | Lean meat | 3 |
| Dietary Fiber, g | 1 | | |
| Protein, g | 31 | | |

# ORANGE-GINGER CHICKEN AND NOODLES

### 5 SERVINGS

*Parboiling dense vegetables such as cauliflower ensures they will be done at the same time as the less dense vegetables. In this recipe, parboiling is conveniently combined with cooking the noodles. If you use frozen caulifowerets, eliminate parboiling; thaw and drain cauliflower before adding to stir-fry.*

**Orange-Ginger Sauce (page 122)**

**1/2 head cauliflower, cut into flowerets (4 cups)**

**1 package (8 ounces) dried Chinese noodles or 8 ounces uncooked linguine or thin spaghetti***

**1 pound skinless boneless chicken breast halves**

**1 clove garlic, finely chopped**

**2 green onions, cut into 1-inch diagonal pieces**

**1 medium green bell pepper, cut into 2 × 1/4-inch strips**

**1 tablespoon chopped fresh cilantro, if desired**

**1/2 medium orange, cut into thin slices, if desired**

Prepare Orange-Ginger Sauce. Heat 6 cups water to boiling in 3-quart saucepan. Add cauliflower. Heat to boiling; reduce heat to medium-low. Cook 2 minutes. Break noodles into 3-inch pieces; add to saucepan. Cook about 3 minutes or just until noodles are tender; drain. Cut chicken into 3/4-inch pieces.

Spray nonstick wok or 12-inch skillet with nonstick cooking spray; heat over medium-high heat until cooking spray starts to bubble. Add chicken; stir-fry about 2 minutes or until brown. Add cauliflower and noodles, garlic, green onions and bell pepper; stir-fry 1 minute. Add sauce; cook and stir until heated through. Sprinkle with cilantro. Garnish with orange slices.

*If using linguine or thin spaghetti, add to boiling water at the same time as cauliflower; cook about 5 minutes or just until tender.

| 1 Serving: | | % Daily Value: | |
|---|---|---|---|
| Calories | 290 | Vitamin A | 2% |
| Calories from fat | 70 | Vitamin C | 36% |
| Fat, g | 8 | Calcium | 4% |
| Saturated, g | 2 | Iron | 10% |
| Cholesterol, mg | 50 | **Diet Exchanges:** | |
| Sodium, mg | 65 | Starch/bread | 2 |
| Carbohydrate, g | 34 | Lean meat | 2 |
| Dietary Fiber, g | 2 | Vegetable | 1 |
| Protein, g | 22 | | |

# CHICKEN SICHUAN WITH SPINACH

### 4 SERVINGS

**1 pound skinless boneless chicken breast halves or thighs**

**1 cup fat-free reduced-sodium chicken broth**

**2 to 3 tablespoons purchased Sichuan sauce or Easy Sichuan Sauce (page 124)**

**2 cloves garlic, finely chopped**

**1/2 teaspoon salt**

**1 1/2 cups 2 × 1/4-inch sticks carrots**

**1 tablespoon cornstarch**

**1 tablespoon water**

**7 ounces spinach, cut into 1/4-inch slices (3 cups)**

Cut chicken into 3/4-inch cubes. Mix broth, Sichuan sauce, garlic and salt in 12-inch wok or skillet. Heat to boiling. Stir in carrots and chicken. Heat to boiling; reduce heat to medium-low. Cover and cook about 10 minutes or until carrots are tender.

Mix cornstarch and water; stir into chicken mixture. Cook about 1 minute, stirring frequently, until thickened. Stir in spinach. Cover and cook about 1 minute or until spinach is wilted.

| 1 Serving: | | % Daily Value: | |
| --- | --- | --- | --- |
| Calories | 170 | Vitamin A | 100% |
| Calories from fat | 35 | Vitamin C | 14% |
| Fat, g | 4 | Calcium | 6% |
| Saturated, g | 1 | Iron | 14% |
| Cholesterol, mg | 60 | **Diet Exchanges:** | |
| Sodium, mg | 560 | Lean meats | 2 |
| Carbohydrate, g | 9 | Vegetables | 2 |
| Dietary Fiber, g | 2 | | |
| Protein, g | 26 | | |

# ORANGE CHICKEN WITH LONG BEANS

### 5 SERVINGS

*Thin Chinese long beans, which grow to as much as a yard long, can be twisted into a wreath for a beautiful presentation. Cut the beans into manageable lengths for forks or chopsticks at the table.*

**1 pound Chinese long beans or whole green beans**

**Garlic Stir-fry Sauce (page 124)***

**1 pound skinless boneless chicken breast halves**

**1 teaspoon grated mandarin orange or tangerine peel**

**1 mandarin orange or tangerine, sectioned and seeds removed**

**1 tablespoon slivered almonds**

Trim ends from beans. Place steamer basket in 1/2 inch water in saucepan or skillet (water should not touch bottom of basket). Form long beans into wreath shape; place beans in basket. Cover and heat to boiling; reduce heat to medium-low. Steam long beans about 3 minutes, green beans 10 to 12 minutes, or until crisp-tender. Carefully transfer wreath to serving platter or arrange green beans in wreath shape on platter; keep warm.

Prepare Garlic Stir-fry Sauce. Cut chicken into 3/4-inch cubes. Spray nonstick wok or 12-inch skillet with nonstick cooking spray; heat over medium-high heat until cooking spray starts to bubble. Add chicken; stir-fry 3 to 4 minutes or until brown and no longer pink in center.

Add stir-fry sauce, broth and orange peel; cook and stir about 1 minute or until hot. Add orange sections; stir until well coated. Place chicken mixture in center of wreath of beans. Sprinkle with almonds.

*1/4 cup purchased stir-fry sauce with garlic and ginger and 1/4 cup fat-free reduced-sodium chicken broth can be substituted for the Garlic Stir-fry Sauce.

| 1 Serving: | | % Daily Value: | |
| --- | --- | --- | --- |
| Calories | 150 | Vitamin A | 6% |
| Calories from fat | 35 | Vitamin C | 10% |
| Fat, g | 4 | Calcium | 6% |
| Saturated, g | 1 | Iron | 8% |
| Cholesterol, mg | 50 | **Diet Exchanges:** | |
| Sodium, mg | 310 | Lean meats | 2 |
| Carbohydrate, g | 10 | Vegetables | 2 |
| Dietary Fiber, g | 3 | | |
| Protein, g | 21 | | |

# SWEET-AND-SOUR CHICKEN

### 6 SERVINGS

*We baked crumb-coated chicken in a very hot oven to keep the crispness of the original deep-fried recipe without the fat. Stir the crisp chicken into the sauce just before serving.*

**1 pound skinless boneless chicken breast halves or thighs**

**1 egg white**

**1 teaspoon water**

**2 tablespoons all-purpose flour**

**2 tablespoons crushed rice crackers, cornmeal or soft bread crumbs**

**1/4 teaspoon baking soda**

**1/4 cup cold water**

**2 tablespoons cornstarch**

**1 can (8 ounces) pineapple chunks in juice, drained and juice reserved**

**1/2 cup sugar**

**1/3 cup seasoned rice vinegar**

**2 teaspoons dark soy sauce**

**1 clove garlic, finely chopped**

**1/4 teaspoon salt**

**2 medium roma (plum) tomatoes, cut into eighths**

**1 medium green bell pepper, cut into 1-inch pieces**

Cut chicken into 3/4-inch pieces. Mix egg white and 1 teaspoon water; toss with chicken in medium glass or plastic bowl. Let stand 10 minutes.

Heat oven to 425°. Spray nonstick cookie sheet with nonstick cooking spray. Mix flour, crushed crackers and baking soda in medium bowl. Remove chicken pieces from egg mixture; dip into flour mixture, turning to coat. Place chicken on cookie sheet; spray with cooking spray about 10 seconds or until surface of chicken appears moist. Bake 10 to 15 minutes, turning once, until brown and no longer pink in center.

Mix 1/4 cup cold water and the cornstarch. Heat reserved pineapple juice, the sugar, vinegar, soy sauce, garlic and salt to boiling in nonstick wok or 12-inch skillet, stirring frequently. Stir in cornstarch mixture; cook and stir about 1 minute or until thickened. Add tomatoes, bell pepper and pineapple; cook and stir 1 minute. Stir in chicken.

| 1 Serving: | | % Daily Value: | |
|---|---|---|---|
| Calories | 235 | Vitamin A | 4% |
| Calories from fat | 45 | Vitamin C | 22% |
| Fat, g | 5 | Calcium | 2% |
| Saturated, g | 2 | Iron | 6% |
| Cholesterol, mg | 40 | **Diet Exchanges:** | |
| Sodium, mg | 310 | Starch/bread | 2 |
| Carbohydrate, g | 32 | Lean meat | 1 |
| Dietary Fiber, g | 1 | | |
| Protein, g | 16 | | |

# CHICKEN ALMOND DING

**6** SERVINGS

4 medium carrots or 16 baby-cut carrots, cut into 1/2-inch slices

1 pound skinless boneless chicken breast halves

1 egg white

1 teaspoon cornstarch

1 teaspoon soy sauce

Dash of white pepper

2 teaspoons cornstarch

2 teaspoons water

1/2 cup fat-free reduced-sodium chicken broth

2 tablespoons oyster sauce or 1 tablespoon dark soy sauce

2 cloves garlic, finely chopped

1 teaspoon finely chopped gingerroot

1 teaspoon vegetable oil

1 cup chopped mushrooms (4 ounces)

1 cup diced celery

1/2 cup diced canned water chestnuts

1/2 teaspoon salt

1 cup frozen green peas

1/2 cup blanched whole almonds, toasted

2 green onions, chopped

Place carrots in boiling water; heat to boiling. Cover and cook 2 minutes. Immediately rinse with cold water; drain. Cut chicken into 1/2-inch pieces. Mix egg white, 1 teaspoon cornstarch, the soy sauce and white pepper in medium glass or plastic bowl. Stir in chicken. Let stand 10 minutes.

Mix 2 teaspoons cornstarch and the water. Mix broth, oyster sauce, garlic and gingerroot.

Spray nonstick wok or 12-inch skillet with nonstick cooking spray; heat over medium-high heat until cooking spray starts to bubble. Add oil; rotate wok to coat side. Add half of the chicken; stir-fry about 2 minutes or until brown. Remove chicken from wok; repeat with remaining chicken.

Return chicken to wok. Add carrots, mushrooms, celery, water chestnuts and salt; stir-fry 1 minute. Stir in broth mixture and peas. Heat to boiling. Stir in cornstarch mixture; cook and stir about 30 seconds or until thickened. Garnish with almonds and green onions.

| 1 Serving: | | % Daily Value: | |
|---|---|---|---|
| Calories | 215 | Vitamin A | 76% |
| Calories from fat | 80 | Vitamin C | 8% |
| Fat, g | 9 | Calcium | 8% |
| Saturated, g | 1 | Iron | 12% |
| Cholesterol, mg | 40 | **Diet Exchanges:** | |
| Sodium, mg | 600 | Lean meat | 2 |
| Carbohydrate, g | 16 | Vegetable | 3 |
| Dietary Fiber, g | 4 | | |
| Protein, g | 22 | | |

# ♥ CHICKEN LO MEIN

### 5 SERVINGS

*Low-fat boiled vegetables and noodles soak up maximum flavor when they are stir-fried in a fresh gingerroot sauce.*

**1/2 pound skinless boneless chicken breast halves**

**1/2 pound snap pea pods, strings removed (2 cups)**

**6 ounces baby-cut carrots, cut lengthwise into 1/4-inch sticks (1 cup)**

**1/2 package (9-ounce size) refrigerated linguine, cut into 2-inch pieces**

**2 teaspoons cornstarch**

**1 teaspoon sugar**

**2 teaspoons water**

**1/3 cup fat-free reduced-sodium chicken broth**

**1 tablespoon soy sauce**

**4 cloves garlic, finely chopped**

**2 teaspoons finely chopped gingerroot**

**Toasted sesame seeds, if desired**

Cut chicken breast halves lengthwise into 2-inch pieces; cut pieces crosswise into 1/2-inch strips. Heat 2 quarts water to boiling in 3-quart saucepan. Add pea pods, carrots and linguine; heat to boiling. Boil 2 to 3 minutes or until linguine is just tender; drain.

Mix cornstarch, sugar and water. Mix broth, soy sauce, garlic and gingerroot; stir in cornstarch mixture.

Spray nonstick wok or 12-inch skillet with nonstick cooking spray; heat over medium-high heat until cooking spray starts to bubble. Add chicken; stir-fry about 2 minutes or until chicken is white. Stir broth mixture; stir into chicken mixture. Stir in pea pods, carrots and linguine. Cook 2 minutes, stirring occasionally. Sprinkle with toasted sesame seeds.

| 1 Serving: | | % Daily Value: | |
|---|---|---|---|
| Calories | 185 | Vitamin A | 52% |
| Calories from fat | 20 | Vitamin C | 18% |
| Fat, g | 2 | Calcium | 4% |
|   Saturated, g | 1 | Iron | 14% |
| Cholesterol, mg | 25 | **Diet Exchanges:** | |
| Sodium, mg | 270 | Starch/bread | 1 1/2 |
| Carbohydrate, g | 29 | Lean meat | 1 |
|   Dietary Fiber, g | 2 | Vegetable | 1 |
| Protein, g | 15 | | |

# ❤ SPICY SHREDDED CHICKEN AND VEGETABLES

### 6 SERVINGS

*Using precut vegetables, such as broccoli slaw or coleslaw mix, is a real time-saver.*

**1/3 cup fat-free reduced-sodium chicken broth**

**1/2 pound skinless boneless chicken breast halves**

**2 cups broccoli slaw or coleslaw mix**

**1/2 medium red bell pepper, cut into 2 × 1/4-inch pieces (1/2 cup)**

**2 tablespoons brown bean sauce***

**2 teaspoons sugar**

**2 teaspoons chile puree with garlic**

**1 teaspoon finely chopped gingerroot**

**4 cups hot cooked rice**

Heat broth to boiling in 10-inch skillet. Add chicken; reduce heat to medium-low. Cover and cook about 8 minutes or until juice of chicken is no longer pink when centers of thickest pieces are cut. Remove chicken from broth; reserve broth. Cool chicken 5 minutes. Cut chicken into 2-inch pieces. Shred pieces with two knives or forks.

Spray nonstick wok or 12-inch skillet with non-stick cooking spray; heat over medium-high heat until cooking spray starts to bubble. Add broccoli slaw; stir-fry about 2 minutes until crisp-tender. Add bell pepper and chicken; stir-fry 1 minute.

Stir bean sauce, sugar, chile puree and gingerroot into reserved broth. Pour into wok; stir-fry about 1 minute or until heated through. Serve over rice.

*Hoisin sauce can be substituted for the brown bean sauce. Decrease sugar to 1 teaspoon.

| 1 Serving: | | % Daily Value: | |
|---|---|---|---|
| Calories | 185 | Vitamin A | 4% |
| Calories from fat | 10 | Vitamin C | 16% |
| Fat, g | 1 | Calcium | 2% |
| Saturated, g | 0 | Iron | 10% |
| Cholesterol, mg | 20 | **Diet Exchanges:** | |
| Sodium, mg | 110 | Starch/bread | 2 |
| Carbohydrate, g | 34 | Vegetable | 1 |
| Dietary Fiber, g | 1 | | |
| Protein, g | 11 | | |

*Spicy Shredded Chicken and Vegetables*

# FIVE-SPICE CHICKEN KABOBS

4 SERVINGS (2 KABOBS EACH)

**1 pound skinless boneless chicken breast halves**

**2 small zucchini, cut into 1-inch chunks**

**16 medium mushrooms**

**1/2 medium red bell pepper, cut into 1-inch squares**

**1 tablespoon packed brown sugar**

**1 tablespoon lemon juice**

**1 tablespoon hoisin sauce**

**1/2 teaspoon five-spice powder**

**1/2 teaspoon grated lemon peel**

**1/4 teaspoon crushed dried red pepper or small hot chile pepper**

**1/4 teaspoon salt**

**1/4 teaspoon sesame oil**

**2 cloves garlic, finely chopped**

**1/4 cup fat-free reduced-sodium chicken broth**

**4 cups hot cooked rice**

Cut chicken into 1-inch pieces. Thread chicken, zucchini, mushrooms and bell pepper alternately on 8-inch skewers, leaving about 1/8-inch space between pieces.*

Mix brown sugar, lemon juice, hoisin sauce, five-spice powder, lemon peel, dried red pepper, salt, sesame oil and garlic. Brush all of marinade on kabobs. Cover and refrigerate at least 1 hour but no longer than 24 hours.

Heat grill or set oven control to broil. Spray grill or broiler pan rack with nonstick cooking spray. Remove kabobs from marinade; reserve marinade. Place kabobs on rack. Grill 3 inches from heat or broil with tops 3 inches from heat 2 minutes. Turn kabobs and brush with marinade. Grill or broil 2 to 3 minutes longer or until chicken is no longer pink in center.

Place remaining marinade in 1-quart saucepan; stir in broth. Heat to boiling over medium heat. Serve kabobs over rice with broth mixture.

*If using wooden skewers, soak in water for at least 30 minutes to prevent burning.

| 2 Kabobs: | | % Daily Value: | |
|---|---|---|---|
| Calories | 380 | Vitamin A | 8% |
| Calories from fat | 45 | Vitamin C | 24% |
| Fat, g | 5 | Calcium | 4% |
| Saturated, g | 2 | Iron | 24% |
| Cholesterol, mg | 60 | **Diet Exchanges:** | |
| Sodium, mg | 230 | Starch/bread | 2 |
| Carbohydrate, g | 56 | Lean meat | 2 |
| Dietary Fiber, g | 3 | Vegetable | 2 |
| Protein, g | 31 | Fruit | 1 |

# FIVE-SPICE TURKEY BREAST

**8** SERVINGS

*(photograph on page 115)*

**8 thin slices gingerroot**

**1/2 teaspoon five-spice powder**

**1 clove garlic, finely chopped**

**2 1/2-pound bone-in turkey breast half with skin**

**1/2 teaspoon sesame oil**

**3 tablespoons hoisin sauce or Chinese barbecue sauce**

**2 teaspoons soy sauce**

**Duck sauce, if desired**

Heat oven to 425°. Spray rack of shallow roasting pan with nonstick cooking spray. Mix gingerroot, five-spice powder and garlic. Loosen turkey skin gently with fingers as far back as possible without tearing skin. Rub gingerroot mixture on turkey under the skin. Secure skin in place with toothpicks. Place turkey on rack in roasting pan; brush skin with sesame oil. Insert meat thermometer in turkey so tip does not touch bone or rest in fat. Roast turkey uncovered about 15 minutes or until brown.

Mix hoisin sauce and soy sauce; pour over turkey. Cover and roast 40 to 45 minutes, brushing once with pan drippings, until meat thermometer reads 170° and juice of turkey is no longer pink when center is cut. Let stand 10 minutes; remove and discard skin. Cut turkey across grain into thin slices; brush with pan drippings. Serve with duck sauce.

| 1 Serving: | | % Daily Value: | |
|---|---|---|---|
| Calories | 155 | Vitamin A | 0% |
| Calories from fat | 35 | Vitamin C | 2% |
| Fat, g | 4 | Calcium | 2% |
| Saturated, g | 1 | Iron | 6% |
| Cholesterol, mg | 65 | **Diet Exchanges:** | |
| Sodium, mg | 150 | Lean meat | 3 |
| Carbohydrate, g | 3 | | |
| Dietary Fiber, g | 0 | | |
| Protein, g | 27 | | |

# ♥ SMOKED TURKEY LO MEIN

**4** SERVINGS

**6 dried black (shiitake) mushrooms**

**1/2 pound fully cooked, smoked, 97 percent fat-free turkey breast, cut into 1/2-inch cubes (1 1/2 cups)**

**1 cup frozen green peas**

**1 package (about 7 ounces) fresh (refrigerated) stir-fry noodles with soy sauce-flavored sauce\***

**3/4 cup water**

**1 tablespoon oyster sauce**

**2 green onions, chopped**

Soak mushrooms in hot water about 20 minutes or until soft; drain. Rinse with warm water; drain. Squeeze out excess moisture. Remove and discard stems; cut caps into thin strips.

Spray nonstick wok or 12-inch skillet with nonstick cooking spray; heat over medium-high heat until cooking spray starts to bubble. Add turkey; stir-fry about 1 minute or until brown. Add the mushrooms, peas, contents of sauce packet from noodles, water and oyster sauce; stir until well mixed. Add noodles; separate and stir-fry about 2 minutes or until heated through.

\*8 ounces dried Chinese noodles and Garlic Stir-fry Sauce (page 124) can be substituted for the stir-fry noodles with sauce; omit water. Cook and drain noodles as directed on package; prepare stir-fry sauce. Add noodles and sauce with mushrooms; stir-fry about 1 minute or until heated through.

| 1 Serving: | | % Daily Value: | |
|---|---|---|---|
| Calories | 225 | Vitamin A | 2% |
| Calories from fat | 25 | Vitamin C | 4% |
| Fat, g | 3 | Calcium | 2% |
| Saturated, g | 0 | Iron | 10% |
| Cholesterol, mg | 45 | **Diet Exchanges:** | |
| Sodium, mg | 540 | Starch/bread | 2 |
| Carbohydrate, g | 29 | Lean meat | 1 1/2 |
| Dietary Fiber, g | 2 | | |
| Protein, g | 23 | | |

# ❤ CHICKEN AND CABBAGE LETTUCE BUNDLES

**6** SERVINGS (2 ROLLS EACH)

**Hot-Sweet Apricot Mustard (page 123) or Lemon Dipping Sauce (page 120)**

**4 dried black (shiitake) mushrooms**

**7 stalks Chinese (napa) cabbage**

**1/2 pound lean ground chicken or turkey, crumbled**

**1 small onion, chopped (1/4 cup)**

**2 tablespoons brown bean sauce**

**1 tablespoon soy sauce**

**1/4 teaspoon five-spice powder**

**12 large leaves iceberg lettuce**

Prepare Hot Mustard or Lemon Dipping Sauce. Soak mushrooms in hot water about 20 minutes or until soft; drain. Rinse with warm water; drain. Squeeze out excess moisture. Remove and discard stems; chop caps. Separate cabbage leaves from stems; chop cabbage, keeping leaves and stems separate.

Spray nonstick wok or 12-inch skillet with non-stick cooking spray; heat over medium-high heat until cooking spray starts to bubble. Add chicken; stir-fry 3 to 4 minutes or until slightly brown. Remove chicken from wok; drain.

Cool wok slightly. Wipe clean; respray and heat over medium-high heat until cooking spray starts to bubble. Add cabbage stems and onion; stir-fry about 2 minutes or until tender. Stir in bean sauce, soy sauce and five-spice powder. Add cabbage leaves, mushrooms and chicken; stir-fry about 1 minute or until heated through and chicken is no longer pink.

To assemble lettuce bundles with Hot Mustard Sauce: Spread a small amount of sauce on each lettuce leaf; place 1/4 cup chicken mixture on center of leaf. Fold in ends; roll up. To assemble with Lemon Dipping Sauce: Place 1/4 cup chicken mixture on each lettuce leaf; drizzle with about 1 teaspoon sauce. Fold in ends; roll up.

| 2 Bundles: | | % Daily Value: | |
|---|---|---|---|
| Calories | 80 | Vitamin A | 12% |
| Calories from fat | 25 | Vitamin C | 14% |
| Fat, g | 3 | Calcium | 6% |
| Saturated, g | 1 | Iron | 8% |
| Cholesterol, mg | 25 | **Diet Exchanges:** | |
| Sodium, mg | 260 | Lean meat | 1 |
| Carbohydrate, g | 4 | Vegetable | 1 |
| Dietary Fiber, g | 1 | | |
| Protein, g | 10 | | |

*Chicken and Cabbage Lettuce Bundles with Hot-Sweet Apricot Mustard*

# 3

# FISH AND SHELLFISH

*Cold Steep-Poached Salmon (page 57)*

## STEAMED SEA BASS

### 3 SERVINGS

*A drawn fish is still whole, but the internal organs have been removed. Remove the scales before steaming a whole fish. Using a fish scaler (available in kitchenware stores), or a short serrated or small dull knife, hold fish under running water and scrape with short, firm strokes working from the tail toward the head; rinse well.*

**1 1/2-pound drawn sea bass or red snapper**

**1 teaspoon grated gingerroot**

**1 teaspoon sesame oil**

**2 tablespoons brown bean sauce**

**2 cloves garlic, finely chopped**

**1/2 teaspoon salt**

**2 teaspoons soy sauce**

**2 green onions**

Rinse fish and pat dry. Slash fish crosswise 3 times on each side. Place on heatproof plate. Mix gingerroot, sesame oil, bean sauce, garlic, salt and soy sauce; rub cavity and outside of fish with mixture. Cover and refrigerate 40 minutes.

Cut green onions into 2-inch pieces; cut pieces lengthwise into thin strips. Place fish on heatproof plate; place plate on rack in steamer. Cover and steam over boiling water in wok or Dutch oven about 15 minutes or until thickest part of fish flakes easily with fork. Garnish with green onions.

| 1 Serving: | | % Daily Value: | |
|---|---|---|---|
| Calories | 200 | Vitamin A | 2% |
| Calories from fat | 35 | Vitamin C | 2% |
| Fat, g | 4 | Calcium | 4% |
| Saturated, g | 1 | Iron | 4% |
| Cholesterol, mg | 105 | **Diet Exchanges:** | |
| Sodium, mg | 810 | Lean meat | 3 |
| Carbohydrate, g | 3 | Vegetable | 1 |
| Dietary Fiber, g | 0 | | |
| Protein, g | 38 | | |

## STEAMED FRAGRANT FISH

### 3 SERVINGS

**2 green onions**

**1 1/2-pound drawn striped bass**

**2 tablespoons dry sherry or rice wine, if desired**

**2 tablespoons soy sauce**

**4 thin slices gingerroot, cut into thin strips**

**1 tablespoon finely shredded orange peel**

**1 tablespoon vegetable oil**

**1 teaspoon sesame oil**

**1 clove garlic, cut in half**

**1/4 cup chopped fresh cilantro leaves**

Cut green onions into 2-inch pieces; cut pieces lengthwise into thin strips. Rinse fish and pat dry. Slash fish crosswise 3 times on each side. Place on heatproof plate. Mix sherry and soy sauce; rub cavity and outside of fish with mixture. Sprinkle gingerroot and orange peel over top of fish.

Place plate with fish on rack in steamer. Cover and steam over boiling water in wok or Dutch oven 15 to 20 minutes or until thickest part of fish flakes easily with fork.

Meanwhile, mix vegetable oil, sesame oil and garlic in 1-quart (or smaller) saucepan. Heat over medium heat just until garlic begins to brown; remove garlic. Sprinkle green onions and cilantro over top of fish. Carefully pour hot oil over entire surface of fish (oil will sizzle). Serve immediately with cooking liquid.

| 1 Serving | | % Daily Value: | |
|---|---|---|---|
| Calories | 300 | Vitamin A | 6% |
| Calories from fat | 125 | Vitamin C | 4% |
| Fat, g | 12 | Calcium | 6% |
| Saturated, g | 3 | Iron | 14% |
| Cholesterol, mg | 100 | **Diet Exchanges:** | |
| Sodium, mg | 800 | Lean meat | 5 |
| Carbohydrate, g | 4 | Vegetable | 1 |
| Dietary Fiber, g | 0 | | |
| Protein, g | 40 | | |

# COLD STEEP-POACHED SALMON

### 4 SERVINGS

*Steep-poaching is a wonderful method to cook mild-flavored fish—it's fat-free and preserves the fish's delicate taste. Be sure to set the timer for the minimum steeping time and test for doneness in the thickest part of the fish. The two dipping sauces—one salty-spicy and the other sweet-crunchy—offer delicious contrasting tastes and textures to complement the salmon.*

**3 thin slices gingerroot**

**3 tablespoons dry sherry, if desired**

**1 pound salmon fillets**

**Cucumber Relish (page 127)**

**1/4 cup Horseradish Dipping Sauce (page 121)**

Mix gingerroot, sherry and enough water to cover fish in 12-inch skillet or Dutch oven. Heat to boiling. Carefully place fish in water. Cover tightly and remove from heat. Let fish steep in hot water 12 to 15 minutes or until fish flakes easily with fork.

Remove fish from poaching liquid. Cover and refrigerate at least 4 hours or until cold. Prepare Cucumber Relish and/or Horseradish Dipping Sauce. Serve with fish.

| 1 Serving: | | % Daily Value: | |
|---|---|---|---|
| Calories | 165 | Vitamin A | 4% |
| Calories from fat | 65 | Vitamin C | 8% |
| Fat, g | 7 | Calcium | 2% |
| Saturated, g | 2 | Iron | 4% |
| Cholesterol, mg | 75 | **Diet Exchanges:** | |
| Sodium, mg | 70 | Lean meat | 3 |
| Carbohydrate, g | 2 | | |
| Dietary Fiber, g | 0 | | |
| Protein, g | 24 | | |

 # RED-COOKED SEA BASS

### 4 SERVINGS

**1 1/4 pounds sea bass, halibut or cod fillets, 1 inch thick**

**3 tablespoons all-purpose flour**

**1 1/2 cups fat-free reduced-sodium chicken broth**

**1/4 cup dry sherry or fat-free reduced-sodium chicken broth**

**1/4 cup mushroom soy sauce**

**1 teaspoon sugar**

**1/2 teaspoon coriander seed**

**4 slices fresh gingerroot**

**2 green onions, cut into 2-inch pieces**

**2 cloves garlic, finely chopped**

**Fresh cilantro sprigs**

Lightly coat fish fillets with flour. Mix remaining ingredients except cilantro.

Spray 12-inch nonstick skillet with nonstick cooking spray; heat over medium-high heat until cooking spray starts to bubble. Cook fish in skillet about 1 1/2 minutes on each side or until light brown; remove from skillet.

Pour broth mixture into skillet. Heat to boiling; reduce heat. Cover and simmer 10 minutes. Add fish to skillet. Heat to boiling; reduce heat. Cover and simmer about 10 minutes, turning once, until fish flakes easily with fork. Serve fish with cooking liquid. Garnish with cilantro.

| 1 Serving: | | % Daily Value: | |
|---|---|---|---|
| Calories | 175 | Vitamin A | 0% |
| Calories from fat | 20 | Vitamin C | 0% |
| Fat, g | 2 | Calcium | 4% |
| Saturated, g | 1 | Iron | 6% |
| Cholesterol, mg | 75 | **Diet Exchanges:** | |
| Sodium, mg | 1310 | Lean meat | 2 |
| Carbohydrate, g | 10 | Vegetable | 2 |
| Dietary Fiber, g | 0 | | |
| Protein, g | 29 | | |

# ♥ GRILLED FISH BUNDLES

### 4 SERVINGS

*Wrapping the marinated fish in cabbage leaves protects it from overcooking on the grill, plus the grilled leaves and onions impart a richer flavor than if the fish were grilled alone. Trim the longest stems from several green onions and use as ties for the fish bundles.*

**Hoisin Dipping Sauce (page 120), if desired**

**1 1/4 pounds turbot, sole or red snapper fillets, 1/2 inch thick**

**3 tablespoons lime juice**

**2 tablespoons soy sauce**

**1 tablespoon grated gingerroot**

**1 tablespoon honey**

**1 teaspoon chile puree with garlic**

**1 teaspoon sesame oil**

**8 large leaves Chinese (napa) cabbage, tough root ends trimmed**

**8 long stems from tops of green onions**

Prepare Hoisin Dipping Sauce. Cut fish into 8 pieces. Mix lime juice, soy sauce, gingerroot, honey, chile puree and sesame oil in medium glass or plastic bowl. Gently stir in fish until coated.

Heat 2 inches water to boiling in 12-inch skillet or Dutch oven. Place 1 cabbage leaf at a time in boiling water 20 seconds. Immediately rinse with cold water; drain on kitchen towel. Place green onion stems in boiling water 20 seconds. Immediately rinse with cold water; drain on kitchen towel.

Remove fish from marinade; reserve marinade. Place 1 piece fish near root end of 1 cabbage leaf. Fold end of leaf over top, then roll until fish is completely wrapped. Lay fish bundle on 1 green onion; lift onion ends and tie around bundle to secure. Repeat with remaining fish, cabbage leaves and green onions. Heat marinade to boiling in 1-quart saucepan. Boil 1 minute; set aside.

Grill fish bundles about 4 inches from heat 10 to 12 minutes, turning once, until fish flakes easily with fork. (To test, cut into center of 1 bundle with tip of knife.) Serve with marinade and/or dipping sauce.

| 1 Serving: | | % Daily Value: | |
|---|---|---|---|
| Calories | 195 | Vitamin A | 6% |
| Calories from fat | 25 | Vitamin C | 10% |
| Fat, g | 3 | Calcium | 6% |
| Saturated, g | 1 | Iron | 6% |
| Cholesterol, mg | 95 | **Diet Exchanges:** | |
| Sodium, mg | 690 | Lean meat | 3 |
| Carbohydrate, g | 8 | Vegetable | 1 |
| Dietary Fiber, g | 1 | | |
| Protein, g | 35 | | |

*Grilled Fish Bundles with Green Onion Brushes and Hoisin Sauce*

# PEKING FISH

### 4 SERVINGS

*The low-fat technique of braise-deglazing is basically stir-frying using very little cooking oil. Use a small amount of water or broth to prevent sticking and ensure food browns attractively.*

**1/2 cup water**

**1/4 cup hoisin sauce**

**2 cloves garlic, finely chopped**

**2 tablespoons grated gingerroot**

**2 tablespoons soy sauce**

**1 tablespoon seasoned rice vinegar**

**2 teaspoons cornstarch**

**1 pound halibut, monkfish or sea bass fillets, 1 inch thick**

**1 teaspoon cornstarch**

**2 teaspoons dry sherry or water**

**1 teaspoon chile oil**

**1 pound broccoli, cut into flowerets and 2 × 1/2-inch pieces (4 cups)**

**3 small carrots, roll-cut (see page 8)**

**1 medium yellow or red bell pepper, cut into 3/4-inch pieces**

**1 small red onion, cut into wedges**

**2 tablespoons water**

Mix 1/2 cup water, the hoisin sauce, garlic, gingerroot, soy sauce, vinegar and 2 teaspoons cornstarch.

Cut fish into 3/4-inch pieces. Mix 1 teaspoon cornstarch and the sherry in medium glass or plastic bowl. Stir in fish until coated.

Spray nonstick wok or 12-inch skillet with nonstick cooking spray; heat over medium-high heat until cooking spray starts to bubble. Add 1/2 teaspoon of the chile oil; rotate wok to coat side. Add fish; stir-fry about 2 1/2 minutes or until fish flakes easily with fork. Remove fish from wok.

Add remaining 1/2 teaspoon chile oil to wok. Add broccoli, carrots, bell pepper, onion and 2 tablespoons water. Cover and cook 5 to 7 minutes, stirring frequently, until vegetables are crisp-tender (add water if necessary to prevent sticking). Stir in hoisin sauce mixture; cook and stir until thickened. Stir in fish; heat through.

| 1 Serving: | | % Daily Value: | |
|---|---|---|---|
| Calories | 185 | Vitamin A | 88% |
| Calories from fat | 35 | Vitamin C | 100% |
| Fat, g | 4 | Calcium | 8% |
| Saturated, g | 1 | Iron | 12% |
| Cholesterol, mg | 60 | **Diet Exchanges:** | |
| Sodium, mg | 650 | Starch/bread | 1 |
| Carbohydrate, g | 21 | Lean meat | 1 1/2 |
| Dietary Fiber, g | 5 | Vegetable | 1 |
| Protein, g | 27 | | |

# BROILED SESAME HALIBUT KABOBS

### 4 SERVINGS

**1 pound halibut or sea bass steaks or fillets, 1 inch thick**

**1 medium zucchini, cut into 1/4-inch slices**

**1 medium yellow summer squash, cut into 1/4-inch slices**

**1/4 teaspoon sugar**

**1 clove garlic, finely chopped**

**2 tablespoons soy sauce**

**1 teaspoon grated gingerroot**

**1 teaspoon sesame oil**

**1 tablespoon sesame seed**

Cut fish into 3/4- to 1-inch pieces. Thread fish, zucchini and squash alternately on each of eight 8-inch skewers.*

Set oven control to broil. Spray broiler pan rack with nonstick cooking spray. Mix sugar, garlic, soy sauce, gingerroot and sesame oil. Brush generously on all sides of kabobs. Sprinkle sesame seed over kabobs. Place kabobs on rack in broiler pan. Broil with tops 4 inches from heat about 3 minutes; turn. Broil about 2 minutes longer or until fish flakes easily with fork.

*If using wooden bamboo skewers, soak in water for 30 minutes before using to prevent burning.

| 1 Serving: | | % Daily Value: | |
|---|---|---|---|
| Calories | 140 | Vitamin A | 4% |
| Calories from fat | 35 | Vitamin C | 6% |
| Fat, g | 4 | Calcium | 4% |
| Saturated, g | 1 | Iron | 6% |
| Cholesterol, mg | 60 | **Diet Exchanges:** | |
| Sodium, mg | 610 | Lean meat | 2 |
| Carbohydrate, g | 4 | Vegetable | 1 |
| Dietary Fiber, g | 1 | | |
| Protein, g | 23 | | |

# KUNG PAO SHRIMP

**4** SERVINGS

*Peanuts still give the signature crunch and big, rich taste of Kung Pao, but our low-fat version bypasses the traditional deep-fried peanuts.*

**1 pound uncooked medium shrimp, peeled and deveined**

**1 teaspoon cornstarch**

**1/4 teaspoon salt**

**1/4 teaspoon white pepper**

**1 teaspoon cornstarch**

**1 tablespoon cold water**

**1 tablespoon dry sherry, if desired**

**1 teaspoon grated gingerroot**

**1/2 teaspoon sugar**

**1/4 teaspoon sesame oil**

**4 cloves garlic, finely chopped**

**1/2 cup partially defatted roasted peanuts or 1/4 cup chopped dry-roasted peanuts**

**1 medium onion, cut into 8 wedges**

**1 large green bell pepper, cut into 3/4-inch pieces**

**2 tablespoons hoisin sauce**

**2 teaspoons chile puree with garlic**

**2 tablespoons chopped green onions**

Toss shrimp, 1 teaspoon cornstarch, the salt and white pepper in medium glass or plastic bowl. Cover and refrigerate 30 minutes.

Mix 1 teaspoon cornstarch, the cold water, sherry, gingerroot, sugar, sesame oil and garlic. Spray nonstick wok or 12-inch skillet with nonstick cooking spray; heat over medium-high heat until cooking spray starts to bubble. Spread peanuts in single layer on paper towel; spray lightly with cooking spray, about 2 seconds. Add to wok; stir-fry about 1 minute or until toasted. Immediately remove from wok; cool.

Spray nonstick wok or 12-inch skillet with cooking spray; heat over medium-high heat until cooking spray starts to bubble. Add onion and bell pepper; stir-fry 1 to 2 minutes or until light brown. Add shrimp; stir-fry just until pink. Add hoisin sauce and chile puree; stir-fry 30 seconds. Stir in cornstarch mixture; cook and stir until thickened. Sprinkle with peanuts and green onions.

| 1 Serving: | | % Daily Value: | |
|---|---|---|---|
| Calories | 175 | Vitamin A | 8% |
| Calories from fat | 45 | Vitamin C | 26% |
| Fat, g | 5 | Calcium | 6% |
| Saturated, g | 0 | Iron | 16% |
| Cholesterol, mg | 160 | **Diet Exchanges:** | |
| Sodium, mg | 430 | Starch/bread | 1/2 |
| Carbohydrate, g | 12 | Lean meat | 2 |
| Dietary Fiber, g | 1 | Vegetable | 1 |
| Protein, g | 22 | | |

# ♥ SICHUAN SHRIMP STIR-FRY

**4** SERVINGS

*Hot chile peppers are a hallmark of Sichuan-style cooking. Jarred chile purees make sauces flavorful as well as spicy. Stir in the fresh jalapeño at the end so it stays bright green and slightly crunchy. The seeds will add more heat, so keep the seeds or discard them to create the just the right amount of heat in the sauce.*

**3/4 pound uncooked medium shrimp, peeled, deveined and cut lengthwise in half**

**1 tablespoon cornstarch**

**2 teaspoons dry sherry or rice wine, if desired**

**1/4 teaspoon salt**

**1 cup fat-free reduced-sodium chicken broth**

**1 1/2 tablespoons soy sauce**

**1 tablespoon chile puree**

**2 teaspoons sugar**

**2 teaspoons grated gingerroot**

**2 teaspoons dry sherry, if desired**

**1 1/2 teaspoons Chinese black vinegar or balsamic vinegar**

**3 cloves garlic, finely chopped**

**1 tablespoon cornstarch**

**1 tablespoon water**

**2 1/2 cups frozen snap pea pods, baby carrot and pearl onion mixture**

**1 cup or canned (drained) baby corn**

**1/2 cup canned whole straw mushrooms, drained**

**1 jalapeño chile, thinly sliced into rings, seeded, if desired**

Mix shrimp, 1 tablespoon cornstarch, 2 teaspoons sherry and the salt in small glass or plastic bowl. Cover and refrigerate at least 20 minutes but no longer than 8 hours.

Mix 1 cup broth, the soy sauce, chile puree, sugar, gingerroot, 2 teaspoons sherry, the vinegar and garlic. Mix 1 tablespoon cornstarch and the water.

Spray nonstick wok or 12-inch skillet with non-stick cooking spray; heat over medium-high heat until cooking spray starts to bubble. Add shrimp; stir-fry 2 to 3 minutes or just until shrimp are pink. Remove shrimp from wok.

Add frozen vegetables to wok; stir-fry 1 minute. Add broth mixture; cover and simmer 5 to 6 minutes or until carrots are tender. Stir in corn and mushrooms. Stir in cornstarch mixture; cook and stir until thickened. Stir in shrimp and chile; heat through.

| 1 Serving: | | % Daily Value: | |
|---|---|---|---|
| Calories | 165 | Vitamin A | 16% |
| Calories from fat | 10 | Vitamin C | 56% |
| Fat, g | 1 | Calcium | 6% |
| Saturated, g | 0 | Iron | 24% |
| Cholesterol, mg | 120 | **Diet Exchanges:** | |
| Sodium, mg | 900 | Starch/bread | 1 |
| Carbohydrate, g | 25 | Lean meat | 1 |
| Dietary Fiber, g | 4 | Vegetable | 2 |
| Protein, g | 18 | | |

*Sichuan Shrimp Stir-Fry*

# ♥ SHRIMP WITH GARLIC SAUCE

**4** SERVINGS

*Slicing the shrimp lengthwise in half makes it possible to stretch a smaller amount—plus the shrimp curls attractively when stir-fried.*

**8 dried black (shiitake) mushrooms**

**2 teaspoons cornstarch**

**1 tablespoon water**

**3/4 pound uncooked medium shrimp, peeled, deveined and cut lengthwise in half**

**3/4 pound green cabbage, cut into 2 × 3/4-inch pieces**

**2 medium carrots, cut into thin diagonal slices**

**1/2 cup fat-free reduced-sodium chicken broth**

**4 cloves garlic, finely chopped**

**4 green onions, cut into 1-inch diagonal pieces**

**1 tablespoon chile puree with garlic**

Soak mushrooms in hot water about 20 minutes or until soft; drain. Rinse with warm water; drain. Squeeze out excess moisture. Remove and discard stems; cut caps into thin strips. Mix cornstarch and water.

Spray nonstick wok or 12-inch skillet with nonstick cooking spray; heat over medium-high heat until cooking spray starts to bubble. Add shrimp; stir-fry just until pink. Remove shrimp from wok.

Cool wok slightly. Respray and heat over medium-high heat until cooking spray starts to bubble. Add mushrooms, cabbage and carrots; stir-fry 1 minute. Add broth and garlic; heat to boiling. Cover and boil 4 minutes.

Stir in cornstarch mixture; cook and stir about 30 seconds or until thickened. Add shrimp, green onions and chile puree; cook and stir about 30 seconds or until shrimp are hot.

| 1 Serving: | | % Daily Value: | |
|---|---|---|---|
| Calories | 115 | Vitamin A | 60% |
| Calories from fat | 10 | Vitamin C | 26% |
| Fat, g | 1 | Calcium | 8% |
| Saturated, g | 0 | Iron | 18% |
| Cholesterol, mg | 120 | **Diet Exchanges:** | |
| Sodium, mg | 270 | Starch/bread | 1/2 |
| Carbohydrate, g | 13 | Lean meat | 1 |
| Dietary Fiber, g | 3 | Vegetable | 1 |
| Protein, g | 16 | | |

*Shrimp with Garlic Sauce*

#  SHRIMP LO MEIN

### 4 SERVINGS

*The low-fat technique of water-velveting fish or poultry is easy and especially delicious with shrimp. We marinated the shrimp in beaten egg white with a little salt and other flavorings. They are then quickly poached in boiling water. The shrimp maintain their tender juiciness with no chance of overcooking to toughness.*

**1 egg white**

**1/4 teaspoon salt**

**2 teaspoons dry sherry, if desired**

**1 teaspoon vegetable oil**

**1 pound uncooked medium shrimp, peeled and deveined**

**1 1/2 tablespoons cornstarch**

**1 cup fat-free reduced-sodium chicken broth**

**3 tablespoons soy sauce**

**1 1/2 tablespoons grated gingerroot**

**1 1/2 teaspoons cornstarch**

**1 package (8 ounces) dried Chinese noodles or 8 ounces uncooked thin spaghetti**

**6 green onions, cut into 3/4-inch pieces**

**6 bok choy stems with leaves, sliced (3 cups)**

**2 medium stalks celery, cut into diagonal slices (1 cup)**

Beat egg white, salt, sherry and oil in medium glass or plastic bowl. Stir in shrimp. Stir in 1 1/2 tablespoons cornstarch. Cover and refrigerate at least 30 minutes but no longer than 8 hours.

Mix broth, soy sauce, gingerroot and 1 1/2 teaspoons cornstarch.

Cook noodles as directed on package; remove noodles from cooking water with tongs and drain well. Stir shrimp into boiling noodle water. Gently stir in circular motion about 2 minutes or just until shrimp are pink; drain.

Spray nonstick wok or 12-inch skillet with nonstick cooking spray; heat over medium-high heat until cooking spray starts to bubble. Add green onions; stir-fry 1 minute. Add bok choy and celery; stir-fry 3 minutes. Add broth mixture; cook and stir 1 1/2 minutes. Stir in noodles and shrimp; heat through.

| 1 Serving: | | % Daily Value: | |
|---|---|---|---|
| Calories | 255 | Vitamin A | 22% |
| Calories from fat | 20 | Vitamin C | 26% |
| Fat, g | 2 | Calcium | 12% |
| Saturated, g | 0 | Iron | 26% |
| Cholesterol, mg | 160 | **Diet Exchanges:** | |
| Sodium, mg | 1280 | Starch/bread | 2 |
| Carbohydrate, g | 39 | Lean meat | 1 |
| Dietary Fiber, g | 2 | Vegetable | 2 |
| Protein, g | 22 | | |

# SHRIMP TOFU CAKE

### 6 SERVINGS

**1 package (14 ounces) firm lite tofu**

**3/4 pound uncooked medium shrimp, peeled, deveined and chopped**

**1/4 cup chopped green onions (3 medium)**

**2 tablespoons cornstarch**

**2 teaspoons sesame oil**

**1/2 teaspoon salt**

**1/4 teaspoon white pepper**

**2 egg whites, slightly beaten**

**Lettuce leaves**

**2 tablespoons oyster sauce**

Heat oven to 375°. Spray square pan, 9 × 9 × 2 inches, with nonstick cooking spray. Mash tofu with fork in medium bowl. Stir in shrimp, green onions, cornstarch, sesame oil, salt, white pepper and egg whites until well mixed. Spread mixture in pan. Bake 25 minutes.

Line serving platter with lettuce leaves. Cut tofu cake into 3-inch squares; place on lettuce leaves. Sprinkle with oyster sauce.

| 1 Serving: | | % Daily Value: | |
|---|---|---|---|
| Calories | 110 | Vitamin A | 8% |
| Calories from fat | 35 | Vitamin C | 4% |
| Fat, g | 4 | Calcium | 16% |
| Saturated, g | 0 | Iron | 48% |
| Cholesterol, mg | 80 | **Diet Exchanges:** | |
| Sodium, mg | 570 | Lean meat | 2 |
| Carbohydrate, g | 5 | Vegetable | 1 |
| Dietary Fiber, g | 2 | | |
| Protein, g | 16 | | |

 EMPEROR'S SHRIMP

**4** SERVINGS

**1 head iceberg lettuce**

**2 green onions**

**1 tablespoon cornstarch**

**1 tablespoon water**

**1 1/2 pounds uncooked large shrimp in shells**

**1 tablespoon garlic (6 cloves), finely chopped**

**1/4 cup ketchup**

**2 teaspoons light soy sauce**

**1/2 cup fat-free reduced-sodium chicken broth**

**1 tablespoon dry white wine or fat-free reduced-sodium chicken broth**

**1 teaspoon sesame oil**

Remove outer leaves from the lettuce until head is about 4 inches in diameter. Remove core; cut 1-inch slice from core end of lettuce and discard. Place lettuce, cut side up, on serving plate.

Cut green onions into 2-inch pieces; cut pieces lengthwise into thin strips. Cover with iced water; let stand about 10 minutes or until strips curl. Mix cornstarch and water. Wash shrimp; pat dry with paper towels.

Spray nonstick wok or 12-inch skillet with nonstick cooking spray; heat over medium-high heat until cooking spray starts to bubble. Add shrimp and garlic; stir-fry about 2 minutes or until shrimp are pink. Remove shrimp from wok; cool slightly. Peel and devein shrimp, leaving tails intact.

Mix ketchup and soy sauce in wok; cook 30 seconds. Stir in broth; heat to boiling. Stir in cornstarch mixture, wine and sesame oil; cook and stir until thickened. Add shrimp; stir-fry until sauce coats shrimp. Hang shrimp, tails down, around edge of lettuce, securing with toothpicks. Drain green onions on paper towel; place green onions in center.

| 1 Serving: | | % Daily Value: | |
|---|---|---|---|
| Calories | 120 | Vitamin A | 6% |
| Calories from fat | 20 | Vitamin C | 4% |
| Fat, g | 2 | Calcium | 4% |
| Saturated, g | 0 | Iron | 16% |
| Cholesterol, mg | 160 | **Diet Exchanges:** | |
| Sodium, mg | 630 | Lean meat | 2 |
| Carbohydrate, g | 8 | Regular meat | 2 |
| Dietary Fiber, g | 0 | | |
| Protein, g | 18 | | |

# SWEET-AND-SOUR SHRIMP

**4** SERVINGS (1 1/2 CUPS EACH)

*This light sauce is more sweet than sour; stir in a little more vinegar if you'd like a tangier sauce.*

**1 egg white**

**1/4 teaspoon salt**

**2 teaspoons dry sherry, if desired**

**1 teaspoon sesame oil**

**1 pound uncooked medium shrimp, peeled and deveined**

**1 1/2 tablespoons cornstarch**

**1 cup fat-free reduced-sodium chicken broth**

**1/3 cup red wine vinegar**

**1 can (8 ounces) pineapple chunks in juice, drained and juice reserved**

**1/3 cup apricot preserves**

**1 teaspoon soy sauce**

**1 1/2 tablespoons cornstarch**

**1 clove garlic, finely chopped**

**3 medium carrots, cut into diagonal slices (1 1/2 cups)**

**2 medium green and/or red bell peppers, cut into 1-inch pieces**

**3 green onions, cut into 2-inch diagonal pieces**

**1 1/2 tablespoons toasted sesame seed**

Beat egg white, salt, sherry and oil in medium glass or plastic bowl. Stir in shrimp. Stir in 1 1/2 tablespoons cornstarch. Cover and refrigerate at least 30 minutes but no longer than 8 hours.

Mix broth, vinegar, reserved pineapple juice, apricot preserves, soy sauce, 1 1/2 tablespoons cornstarch and the garlic.

Heat 6 cups water to boiling in 4-quart saucepan. Stir in shrimp. Gently stir in circular motion about 2 minutes or just until shrimp are pink; drain.

Spray nonstick wok or 12-inch skillet with non-stick cooking spray; heat over medium-high heat until cooking spray starts to bubble. Add carrots and bell peppers; cover and cook 3 minutes (add a small amount of water if necessary to prevent sticking). Add green onions; stir-fry about 3 minutes or until vegetables are crisp-tender.

Stir in broth mixture; heat to boiling. Boil about 1 minute, stirring constantly, until thickened. Stir in pineapple and shrimp until coated with sauce; heat through. Garnish with sesame seed.

| 1 Serving: | | % Daily Value: | |
|---|---|---|---|
| Calories | 270 | Vitamin A | 80% |
| Calories from fat | 35 | Vitamin C | 50% |
| Fat, g | 4 | Calcium | 8% |
| Saturated, g | 1 | Iron | 22% |
| Cholesterol, mg | 160 | **Diet Exchanges:** | |
| Sodium, mg | 560 | Lean meat | 2 |
| Carbohydrate, g | 42 | Vegetable | 2 |
| Dietary Fiber, g | 4 | Fruit | 2 |
| Protein, g | 21 | | |

# ♥ SCALLOPS WITH BLACK BEAN SAUCE

**4** SERVINGS

*For a more elegant presentation, cut sea scallops horizontally in half and crosscut the tops; steam until tops open up like a flower and scallops are white in center. Arrange on julienned vegetables and top with sauce.*

**Black Bean Sauce (page 125)**

**2 medium carrots**

**1/4 pound Chinese pea pods (1 cup)**

**1 small leek**

**1 pound sea or bay scallops**

**1/4 teaspoon salt**

**2 green onions, sliced**

**Fresh cilantro sprigs, if desired**

Prepare Black Bean Sauce. Cut carrots crosswise into 2 1/2-inch pieces. Remove strings from pea pods; stack and cut into thin julienne strips. Cut leek lengthwise in half and rinse carefully. Cut leek crosswise into 2-inch pieces; cut pieces lengthwise into thin julienne strips. If using sea scallops, cut in half.

Spray nonstick wok or 12-inch skillet with nonstick cooking spray; heat over medium-high heat until cooking spray starts to bubble. Add carrots, pea pods, leek and salt; stir-fry about 3 minutes or until carrots are crisp-tender. Remove vegetables from wok to serving platter; keep warm.

Cool wok slightly. Respray and heat over medium-high heat until cooking spray starts to bubble. Add scallops; stir-fry about 2 minutes or until white in center. Spoon scallops onto vegetables. Drizzle with warm bean sauce. Sprinkle with green onions and cilantro. Garnish with cilantro.

| 1 Serving: | | % Daily Value: | |
|---|---|---|---|
| Calories | 200 | Vitamin A | 62% |
| Calories from fat | 20 | Vitamin C | 22% |
| Fat, g | 2 | Calcium | 18% |
| Saturated, g | 0 | Iron | 30% |
| Cholesterol, mg | 35 | **Diet Exchanges:** | |
| Sodium, mg | 1050 | Starch/bread | 1 |
| Carbohydrate, g | 20 | Lean meat | 2 |
| Dietary Fiber, g | 3 | Vegetable | 1 |
| Protein, g | 29 | | |

# ♥ ORANGE SCALLOPS AND PEA PODS

### 4 SERVINGS

*Dried tangerine peel, a Chinese seasoning available at Asian markets, can be substituted for the orange peel. Use tangerine or mandarin orange juice for the orange juice.*

1 pound sea or bay scallops

2 cloves garlic, finely chopped

1 teaspoon cornstarch

1/4 teaspoon salt

1/8 teaspoon white pepper

1/8 teaspoon sesame oil

1 teaspoon grated orange peel

1/2 cup orange juice

1/4 cup fat-free reduced-sodium chicken broth

1/4 cup rice wine, sweet white wine or fat-free reduced-sodium chicken broth

1 tablespoon soy sauce

2 teaspoons cornstarch

1 1/2 teaspoons honey

3/4 teaspoon grated gingerroot

1/2 pound Chinese pea pods, strings removed (2 cups)

Sliced green onions, if desired

Chopped cashews, if desired

If using sea scallops, cut in half. Mix scallops, garlic, 1 teaspoon cornstarch, the salt, white pepper and sesame oil in medium glass or plastic bowl. Cover and refrigerate 30 minutes.

Mix orange peel, orange juice, broth, rice wine, soy sauce, 2 teaspoons cornstarch, the honey and gingerroot.

Spray nonstick wok or 12-inch skillet with nonstick cooking spray; heat over medium-high heat until cooking spray starts to bubble. Add pea pods; stir-fry 1 to 2 minutes or until bright green. Remove pea pods from wok. Add scallops to wok; stir-fry about 2 minutes or until white in center. Remove scallops from wok.

Add orange juice mixture to wok; heat to boiling. Cook, stirring constantly, until thickened. Stir in scallops and pea pods until coated; heat through. Garnish with green onions and cashews.

| 1 Serving: | | % Daily Value: | |
|---|---|---|---|
| Calories | 170 | Vitamin A | 6% |
| Calories from fat | 20 | Vitamin C | 10% |
| Fat, g | 2 | Calcium | 14% |
| Saturated, g | 0 | Iron | 20% |
| Cholesterol, mg | 35 | **Diet Exchanges:** | |
| Sodium, mg | 720 | Lean meat | 2 |
| Carbohydrate, g | 12 | Fruit | 1 |
| Dietary Fiber, g | 0 | | |
| Protein, g | 26 | | |

# ♥ SHELLFISH SAND POT

**4** SERVINGS

*A "sandy" pot or clay pot refers to a Chinese earthenware casserole that is used for "clear-simmered" (without soy sauce) dishes. By slowly cooking in richly flavored broth, the natural flavors of food are retained. The porcelain or clay of a traditional sand pot prevents evaporation of the cooking liquid and the food is usually served directly from the casserole. For shellfish, the technique is quicker and just as tasty. Here a Dutch oven stands in for the clay casserole. The accompaniment of choice is barley, a grain first cultivated in China and still served in provincial Chinese cooking.*

1 1/4 pounds clams, scrubbed

1 1/4 pounds mussels, scrubbed and debearded

2 slices turkey bacon, diced (2 tablespoons)

1 1/2 teaspoons fermented black beans, rinsed, drained and mashed

1 teaspoon grated gingerroot

3 cloves garlic, finely chopped

1 large fennel bulb, trimmed, cut in half and thinly sliced

1 small red bell pepper, cut into strips

1 medium carrot, cut into thin diagonal slices

1 cup frozen pearl onions, thawed

2 tablespoons water

1 cup fat-free reduced-sodium chicken broth

1/4 cup dry sherry or fat-free reduced-sodium chicken broth

2 tablespoons soy sauce

1 teaspoon sugar

1 teaspoon grated lemon peel

1 teaspoon lemon juice

1 teaspoon chile puree with garlic

4 green onions, cut into 1-inch pieces

Hot cooked barley, hot cooked rice or garlic toast, if desired

Discard any clams or mussels that are broken or open (dead). Cook bacon in Dutch oven over medium-high heat, stirring occasionally, until crisp; drain. Remove bacon from Dutch oven. Add black beans, gingerroot and garlic; stir-fry 30 seconds.

Add fennel, bell pepper, carrot, pearl onions and water; stir-fry about 2 minutes or until vegetables are crisp-tender. Stir in bacon, broth, sherry, soy sauce, sugar, lemon peel, lemon juice and chile puree; cook 1 minute.

Stir in clams, mussels and green onions. Cover tightly and heat to simmering over medium-high heat. Simmer 4 to 5 minutes or just until shellfish open (if mussels open before clams, remove and keep warm). Discard any unopened mussels or clams. Serve mixture ladled over barley.

| 1 Serving: | | % Daily Value: | |
|---|---|---|---|
| Calories | 130 | Vitamin A | 42% |
| Calories from fat | 20 | Vitamin C | 38% |
| Fat, g | 2 | Calcium | 10% |
| Saturated, g | 1 | Iron | 30% |
| Cholesterol, mg | 30 | **Diet Exchanges:** | |
| Sodium, mg | 920 | Starch/bread | 1 |
| Carbohydrate, g | 18 | Lean meat | 1 |
| Dietary Fiber, g | 3 | | |
| Protein, g | 13 | | |

# ♥ VELVET CRABMEAT

**4** SERVINGS

*Velvet refers to the soft texture of the cooked egg whites. Blanching longer-cooking vegetables, such as broccoli, partially cooks them, so stir-frying time is reduced, along with the amount of oil needed for cooking.*

**1 1/2 pounds broccoli**

**1/2 pound frozen cooked crabmeat, thawed**

**8 egg whites**

**1/4 cup skim milk**

**1/2 teaspoon salt**

**1/8 teaspoon white pepper**

**1 teaspoon rice wine or sweet white wine, if desired**

**1 teaspoon soy sauce**

**1 teaspoon sesame oil**

**1/2 teaspoon salt**

**2 cloves garlic, finely chopped**

Heat oven to 175°. Cut flowerets from broccoli stems. Peel broccoli stems. Cut stems lengthwise into 1-inch strips. Cut strips into 1/4-inch diagonal slices. Place broccoli flowerets and stems in boiling water; cook uncovered 1 minute. Immediately rinse with cold water; drain. Drain crabmeat thoroughly; remove cartilage. Squeeze out excess moisture from crabmeat.

Beat egg whites, milk, 1/2 teaspoon salt and the white pepper until foamy. Mix wine, soy sauce and 1/2 teaspoon of the sesame oil.

Spray nonstick wok or 12-inch skillet with nonstick cooking spray; heat over medium-high heat until cooking spray starts to bubble. Add remaining 1/2 teaspoon sesame oil, the broccoli and 1/2 teaspoon salt; stir-fry 1 minute. Remove broccoli from wok; place on heatproof platter. Keep warm in oven.

Wash and thoroughly dry wok. Respray and heat over medium-high heat until cooking spray starts to bubble. Add garlic and egg white mixture; stir-fry 10 seconds. (Egg whites should not be firm before adding crabmeat.) Add crabmeat and wine mixture; cook and stir about 2 minutes or until egg white mixture is firm (do not overcook). Pour crabmeat mixture over broccoli.

| 1 Serving: | | % Daily Value: | |
|---|---|---|---|
| Calories | 125 | Vitamin A | 14% |
| Calories from fat | 20 | Vitamin C | 82% |
| Fat, g | 2 | Calcium | 12% |
| Saturated, g | 0 | Iron | 8% |
| Cholesterol, mg | 55 | **Diet Exchanges:** | |
| Sodium, mg | 910 | Lean meat | 2 |
| Carbohydrate, g | 8 | Vegetable | 1 |
| Dietary Fiber, g | 2 | | |
| Protein, g | 21 | | |

*Velvet Crabmeat*

# 4

# BEEF, PORK AND VEAL

*Canton Beef (page 82)*

# ♥ QUICK BEEF TIPS AND VEGETABLES

### 4 SERVINGS

*This fast family meal uses purchased stir-fry sauce and precut frozen vegetables to cut preparation time. Look for snap pea pods rather than snow pea pods when using frozen stir-fry vegetables, as snap pea pods retain their crispness through freezing and stir-frying.*

**1/2 pound beef boneless sirloin tip steak**

**1 package (16 ounces) frozen mixed vegetables with snap pea pods**

**1 tablespoon water**

**1/4 cup stir-fry sauce with garlic and ginger**

**2 cups hot cooked rice**

Trim fat from beef. Cut beef into 1/2-inch cubes. Spray nonstick wok or 12-inch skillet with nonstick cooking spray; heat over medium-high heat until cooking spray starts to bubble. Add beef; stir-fry about 2 minutes or until brown. Add vegetables and water; stir-fry 1 minute.

Stir in stir-fry sauce until well mixed; reduce heat to medium. Cover and cook 5 to 7 minutes, stirring frequently, until vegetables are crisp-tender. Serve over rice.

| 1 Serving: | | % Daily Value: | |
|---|---|---|---|
| Calories | 210 | Vitamin A | 14% |
| Calories from fat | 25 | Vitamin C | 30% |
| Fat, g | 3 | Calcium | 4% |
| Saturated, g | 1 | Iron | 16% |
| Cholesterol, mg | 25 | **Diet Exchanges:** | |
| Sodium, mg | 740 | Starch/bread | 2 |
| Carbohydrate, g | 34 | Lean meat | 1 |
| Dietary Fiber, g | 3 | Vegetable | 1 |
| Protein, g | 15 | | |

# GRILLED BEEF STRIPS ORIENTAL

### 4 SERVINGS (ABOUT 6 PIECES EACH)

*Have leftovers? Make them into a quick and delicious chilled Oriental beef salad.*

**Hot Mustard Sauce (page 123) or Lemon Dipping Sauce (page 120)**

**1 pound beef boneless sirloin or top round steak**

**1 tablespoon ground ginger**

**1 teaspoon five-spice powder**

**1 teaspoon ground mustard (dry)**

**1/4 teaspoon salt**

Prepare Hot Mustard Sauce and/or Lemon Dipping Sauce. Trim fat from beef. Cut beef lengthwise into 3- to 4-inch strips; cut strips crosswise into 1/4-inch slices. Mix ginger, five-spice powder, mustard and salt in medium bowl; stir in beef. Let stand 5 minutes.

Heat grill or set oven control to broil. Spray grill rack or broiler pan rack with nonstick cooking spray. Place beef on rack. Grill 3 inches from heat or broil with tops 3 inches from heat 2 to 3 minutes. Turn beef. Grill or broil about 2 minutes longer or until brown and cooked to desired doneness. Serve with one or both sauces for dipping.

| 1 Serving: | | % Daily Value: | |
|---|---|---|---|
| Calories | 135 | Vitamin A | 0% |
| Calories from fat | 45 | Vitamin C | 0% |
| Fat, g | 5 | Calcium | 2% |
| Saturated, g | 1 | Iron | 12% |
| Cholesterol, mg | 55 | **Diet Exchanges:** | |
| Sodium, mg | 170 | Lean meat | 2 1/2 |
| Carbohydrate, g | 2 | | |
| Dietary Fiber, g | 0 | | |
| Protein, g | 21 | | |

# ❤ SPICY BEEF WITH PEA PODS

**4** SERVINGS

*When time allows, marinate the meat overnight in the refrigerator to develop a deeper, more beefy flavor without the use of any oil for stir-frying.*

**1/2 pound beef boneless sirloin steak**

**1 teaspoon cornstarch**

**2 teaspoons soy sauce**

**1/2 cup fat-free reduced-sodium chicken broth**

**2 cloves garlic, finely chopped**

**1 teaspoon soy sauce**

**2 teaspoons cornstarch**

**2 teaspoons cold water**

**1/2 pound Chinese pea pods, strings removed (2 cups)**

**1 can (14 to 15 ounces) baby corn, drained**

**1 hot red chili, finely chopped (1 tablespoon)**

**2 cups hot cooked rice**

Trim fat from beef. Cut beef lengthwise into 2-inch pieces; cut pieces crosswise into 1/8-inch slices. Toss beef, 1 teaspoon cornstarch and 2 teaspoons soy sauce. Let stand 10 minutes, or cover and refrigerate no longer than 24 hours.

Mix broth, garlic and 1 teaspoon soy sauce in medium bowl. Mix 2 teaspoons cornstarch and the cold water; stir into broth mixture.

Spray nonstick wok or 12-inch skillet with non-stick cooking spray; heat over medium-high heat until cooking spray starts to bubble. Add beef; stir-fry 2 to 3 minutes or until brown. Remove beef from wok.

Cool wok slightly. Wipe clean; respray and heat over medium-high heat until cooking spray starts to bubble. Add pea pods, corn and chili; stir-fry about 1 minute or until pea pods are bright green. Stir in beef. Stir broth mixture; stir into beef mixture. Cook and stir 1 to 2 minutes or until sauce is thickened and clear and pea pods are crisp-tender. Serve over rice.

| 1 Serving: | | % Daily Value: | |
|---|---|---|---|
| Calories | 265 | Vitamin A | 4% |
| Calories from fat | 25 | Vitamin C | 38% |
| Fat, g | 3 | Calcium | 4% |
| Saturated, g | 1 | Iron | 22% |
| Cholesterol, mg | 25 | **Diet Exchanges:** | |
| Sodium, mg | 610 | Starch/bread | 2 |
| Carbohydrate, g | 46 | Lean meat | 1 |
| Dietary Fiber, g | 3 | Vegetable | 3 |
| Protein, g | 17 | | |

# BEEF AND BROCCOLI WITH GARLIC SAUCE

### 4 SERVINGS

*By using a nonstick pan and nonstick cooking spray, it's not necessary to add any oil to stir-fry the sirloin.*

**1/2 pound beef boneless sirloin or round steak**

**1/4 teaspoon salt**

**Dash of white pepper**

**1 pound broccoli, cut into flowerets and 1 × 1/2-inch pieces (4 cups)**

**1 teaspoon cornstarch**

**1 teaspoon soy sauce**

**1 teaspoon sesame oil**

**1/4 cup fat-free reduced-sodium chicken broth**

**1 teaspoon vegetable oil**

**1 tablespoon finely chopped garlic (6 cloves)**

**1 teaspoon finely chopped gingerroot**

**2 tablespoons brown bean paste**

**1 can (8 ounces) sliced bamboo shoots, drained**

**2 cups hot cooked rice**

Trim fat from beef. Cut beef lengthwise into 2-inch strips. Cut strips crosswise into 1/8-inch slices. Toss beef with salt and white pepper. Place broccoli in 1 inch boiling water; heat to boiling. Cover and cook 2 minutes. Immediately rinse with cold water; drain.

Mix cornstarch and soy sauce; stir in sesame oil and broth. Spray nonstick wok or 12-inch skillet with nonstick cooking spray; heat over medium-high heat until cooking spray starts to bubble. Add beef; stir-fry about 2 minutes or until brown. Remove beef from wok.

Cool wok slightly. Wipe clean and respray. Add oil and rotate wok to coat side. Heat over medium-high heat. Add garlic, gingerroot and bean paste; stir-fry 30 seconds. Add bamboo shoots; stir-fry 20 seconds. Stir in beef and broccoli. Stir in corn-starch mixture; cook and stir about 30 seconds or until thickened. Serve over rice.

| 1 Serving: | | % Daily Value: | |
|---|---|---|---|
| Calories | 215 | Vitamin A | 8% |
| Calories from fat | 45 | Vitamin C | 54% |
| Fat, g | 5 | Calcium | 4% |
| Saturated, g | 1 | Iron | 14% |
| Cholesterol, mg | 25 | **Diet Exchanges:** | |
| Sodium, mg | 270 | Starch/bread | 2 |
| Carbohydrate, g | 30 | Lean meat | 1 |
| Dietary Fiber, g | 3 | | |
| Protein, g | 15 | | |

*Beef and Broccoli with Garlic Sauce*

## ♥ CANTON BEEF

### 4 SERVINGS

*(photograph on page 77)*

**1/2 pound beef boneless sirloin tip steak**

**3/4 cup fat-free reduced-sodium chicken broth**

**1 tablespoon finely chopped garlic (6 cloves)**

**1 tablespoon finely chopped gingerroot**

**1 tablespoon dark soy sauce**

**2 teaspoons packed brown sugar**

**1/2 teaspoon five-spice powder**

**1 tablespoon cornstarch**

**1 tablespoon cold water**

**1 package (16 ounces) frozen stir-fry bell peppers and onions, thawed and drained**

**2 cups cooked brown rice**

Trim fat from beef. Cut beef lengthwise into 2-inch strips; cut strips crosswise into 1/8-inch slices. Mix broth, garlic, gingerroot, soy sauce, brown sugar and five-spice powder in medium glass or plastic bowl. Mix cornstarch and cold water; stir into broth mixture. Stir in beef until evenly coated. Let stand 10 minutes.

Drain beef; reserve marinade. Spray nonstick wok or 12-inch skillet with nonstick cooking spray; heat over medium-high heat until cooking spray starts to bubble. Add beef; stir-fry 2 minutes. Stir in bell peppers and onions and reserved marinade; reduce heat to medium. Cover and cook 3 to 5 minutes, stirring frequently, until sauce is thickened. Serve over rice.

| 1 Serving: | | % Daily Value: | |
|---|---|---|---|
| Calories | 265 | Vitamin A | 2% |
| Calories from fat | 25 | Vitamin C | 28% |
| Fat, g | 3 | Calcium | 4% |
| Saturated, g | 1 | Iron | 12% |
| Cholesterol, mg | 25 | **Diet Exchanges:** | |
| Sodium, mg | 370 | Starch/bread | 2 |
| Carbohydrate, g | 48 | Lean meat | 1 |
| Dietary Fiber, g | 4 | Vegetable | 2 |
| Protein, g | 15 | Fruit | 1/2 |

## ♥ SICHUAN BEEF WITH RICE STICKS

### 4 SERVINGS

*Serve chilled spiced peaches with this spicy Sichuan dish as a refreshing contrast to its heat.*

**1/3 package (6-ounce size) rice stick noodles**

**1/2 pound beef boneless sirloin**

**2 tablespoons chile puree with garlic**

**2 tablespoons soy sauce**

**1 tablespoon finely chopped gingerroot**

**1 teaspoon vegetable oil**

**3 large mushrooms, sliced**

**1/2 head Chinese (napa) cabbage, shredded (3 cups)**

**2 green onions, sliced**

Cook and drain noodles as directed on package. Cut into 2-inch pieces. Trim fat from beef. Cut beef lengthwise into 2-inch strips; cut strips crosswise into 1/8-inch slices.

Spray nonstick wok or 12-inch skillet with nonstick cooking spray; heat over medium-high heat until cooking spray starts to bubble. Add beef; stir-fry 2 to 3 minutes or until brown.

Add chile puree, soy sauce, gingerroot and oil; stir until well mixed. Add mushrooms, cabbage and green onions; stir-fry 1 to 2 minutes or until cabbage is crisp-tender. Serve over noodles.

| 1 Serving: | | % Daily Value: | |
|---|---|---|---|
| Calories | 110 | Vitamin A | 16% |
| Calories from fat | 25 | Vitamin C | 22% |
| Fat, g | 3 | Calcium | 6% |
| Saturated, g | 1 | Iron | 10% |
| Cholesterol, mg | 25 | **Diet Exchanges:** | |
| Sodium, mg | 660 | Lean meat | 1 |
| Carbohydrate, g | 10 | Vegetable | 2 |
| Dietary Fiber, g | 1 | | |
| Protein, g | 12 | | |

*Sichuan Beef with Rice Sticks*

# BEEF AND ASPARAGUS WITH NOODLES

### 4 SERVINGS

1/2 pound beef boneless eye of round steak

1 egg white

1 teaspoon cornstarch

1 teaspoon sesame oil

1/8 teaspoon white pepper

1 package (11.25 ounces) fresh (refrigerated) Chinese noodles or 8 ounces uncooked angel hair pasta

2 cups frozen asparagus cuts, thawed

1/2 medium red bell pepper, cut into 1 × 1/4-inch strips (3/4 cup)

1/3 cup stir-fry sauce with garlic and ginger

Trim fat from beef. Cut beef into 1/2-inch cubes. Mix egg white, cornstarch, sesame oil and white pepper in medium glass or plastic bowl. Stir in beef. Let stand 10 minutes. Cook and drain noodles as directed on package; keep warm.

Spray nonstick wok or 12-inch skillet with non-stick cooking spray; heat over medium-high heat until cooking spray starts to bubble. Add beef; stir-fry about 3 minutes or until brown. Add asparagus and bell pepper; stir-fry 2 to 3 minutes until vegetables are crisp-tender. Add stir-fry sauce; stir-fry about 1 minute or until heated through. Serve over noodles.

| 1 Serving: | | % Daily Value: | |
|---|---|---|---|
| Calories | 370 | Vitamin A | 0% |
| Calories from fat | 35 | Vitamin C | 0% |
| Fat, g | 4 | Calcium | 2% |
| Saturated, g | 1 | Iron | 22% |
| Cholesterol, mg | 25 | **Diet Exchanges:** | |
| Sodium, mg | 35 | Starch/bread | 4 |
| Carbohydrate, g | 64 | Lean meat | 1 |
| Dietary Fiber, g | 2 | Vegetable | 1 |
| Protein, g | 22 | | |

# SICHUAN BEEF AND BEAN SPROUTS

### 4 SERVINGS

1 pound beef boneless eye of round steak

1/4 cup fat-free reduced-sodium chicken broth

1 tablespoon soy sauce

1 tablespoon purchased Sichuan sauce or Easy Sichuan Sauce (page 124)

1/8 teaspoon crushed dried chile peppers

4 roma (plum) tomatoes, cut into eighths

2 cups bean sprouts (4 ounces)

1 tablespoon chopped fresh cilantro

Trim fat from beef. Cut beef lengthwise into 2-inch strips; cut strips crosswise into 1/8-inch slices. Mix broth, soy sauce, Sichuan sauce and chile peppers in medium bowl. Stir in beef. Let stand 10 minutes.

Drain beef; reserve marinade. Spray nonstick wok or 12-inch skillet with nonstick cooking spray; heat over medium-high heat until cooking spray starts to bubble. Add half of the beef; stir-fry 2 to 3 minutes or until brown. Remove beef from wok. Repeat with remaining beef. Return beef to wok.

Add reserved marinade, the tomatoes and bean sprouts to wok; stir-fry about 1 minute or until vegetables are warm. Sprinkle with cilantro.

| 1 Serving: | | % Daily Value: | |
|---|---|---|---|
| Calories | 190 | Vitamin A | 6% |
| Calories from fat | 55 | Vitamin C | 20% |
| Fat, g | 6 | Calcium | 4% |
| Saturated, g | 2 | Iron | 18% |
| Cholesterol, mg | 55 | **Diet Exchanges:** | |
| Sodium, mg | 340 | Lean meat | 3 |
| Carbohydrate, g | 10 | Vegetable | 2 |
| Dietary Fiber, g | 2 | | |
| Protein, g | 26 | | |

# MANDARIN BEEF

### 4 SERVINGS

3/4 pound beef boneless round steak

1 egg white

2 teaspoons cornstarch

1 teaspoon dark soy sauce

1/2 teaspoon sugar

1/8 teaspoon white pepper

1 tablespoon vegetable oil

1 cup shredded carrots (1 1/2 medium)

1 large green bell pepper, cut into
    2 × 1/8-inch strips

2 cloves garlic, finely chopped

1 teaspoon finely chopped gingerroot

1 teaspoon chile puree

1 teaspoon dark soy sauce

2 green onions, chopped

Trim fat from beef. Shred beef (see page 8). Mix egg white, cornstarch, 1 teaspoon soy sauce, the sugar and white pepper in medium glass or plastic bowl. Stir in beef. Let stand 10 minutes.

Spray nonstick wok or 12-inch skillet with non-stick cooking spray; heat over medium-high heat until cooking spray starts to bubble. Add oil; rotate wok to coat side. Add beef; stir-fry 3 to 4 minutes or until brown. Add carrots, bell pepper, garlic and gingerroot; stir-fry 1 minute. Stir in chile puree, 1 teaspoon soy sauce and the green onions; cook and stir 30 seconds.

| 1 Serving: | | % Daily Value: | |
|---|---|---|---|
| Calories | 150 | Vitamin A | 44% |
| Calories from fat | 55 | Vitamin C | 22% |
| Fat, g | 6 | Calcium | 2% |
| Saturated, g | 1 | Iron | 10% |
| Cholesterol, mg | 40 | **Diet Exchanges:** | |
| Sodium, mg | 240 | Lean meat | 2 |
| Carbohydrate, g | 8 | Vegetable | 2 |
| Dietary Fiber, g | 1 | | |
| Protein, g | 17 | | |

# ♥ EASY BEEF LO MEIN

### 5 SERVINGS

1/2 pound beef flank steak

2 green onions

2 cups baby-cut carrots, cut lengthwise into
    1/2-inch sticks

1/2 package (8-ounce size) dried Chinese
    noodles

1 can (8 ounces) sliced bamboo shoots,
    drained

1/3 cup stir-fry sauce with garlic and ginger

1/4 cup water

Trim fat from beef. Cut beef with grain into 2-inch strips; cut strips across grain into 1/8-inch slices. Cut onion tops into 2-inch pieces; cut pieces lengthwise into thin strips. Chop white part of onions.

Heat 6 cups water to boiling in 3-quart saucepan. Add carrots. Cover and cook about 7 minutes or until crisp-tender. Break noodles into 3-inch pieces; stir into boiling water with carrots. Cook uncovered 3 minutes, stirring frequently to separate noodles; drain.

Spray nonstick wok or 12-inch skillet with non-stick cooking spray; heat over medium-high heat until cooking spray starts to bubble. Add beef and chopped onions; stir-fry 2 to 3 minutes or until beef is brown. Add bamboo shoots, noodles and carrots. Stir in stir-fry sauce and water. Cook and stir about 2 minutes or until heated through. Sprinkle with green onion tops.

| 1 Serving: | | % Daily Value: | |
|---|---|---|---|
| Calories | 145 | Vitamin A | 76% |
| Calories from fat | 25 | Vitamin C | 4% |
| Fat, g | 3 | Calcium | 2% |
| Saturated, g | 1 | Iron | 8% |
| Cholesterol, mg | 25 | **Diet Exchanges:** | |
| Sodium, mg | 280 | Starch/bread | 1 |
| Carbohydrate, g | 21 | Lean meat | 1 |
| Dietary Fiber, g | 2 | Vegetable | 1 |
| Protein, g | 11 | | |

# STIR-FRIED BEEF WITH ZUCCHINI

**4** SERVINGS

*Not only do thin slices of meat cook faster, they look more plentiful on the plate! To slice meats thinly, place in freezer fifteen minutes or just until firm but not frozen.*

**1/2 pound beef flank steak**

**1 teaspoon soy sauce**

**Dash of white pepper**

**1 small onion, cut into thin slices (1/2 cup)**

**5 small zucchini (1 pound), cut into 1/4-inch slices (3 1/2 cups)**

**1/2 medium red bell pepper, cut into 1/4-inch slices (1/2 cup)**

**1 teaspoon finely chopped gingerroot**

**2 cloves garlic, finely chopped**

**1/2 cup fat-free reduced-sodium chicken broth**

**1 tablespoon soy sauce**

**1 tablespoon cornstarch**

**1 tablespoon cold water**

**2 cups hot cooked rice**

Trim fat from beef. Cut beef with grain into 2-inch strips; cut strips across grain into 1/8-inch slices. Toss beef, 1 teaspoon soy sauce and the white pepper. Let stand 10 minutes.

Spray nonstick wok or 12-inch skillet with nonstick cooking spray; heat over medium-high heat until cooking spray starts to bubble. Add beef and onion; stir-fry about 2 minutes or until beef is brown. Remove beef mixture from wok.

Cool wok slightly. Wipe clean; respray and heat over medium-high heat until cooking spray starts to bubble. Add zucchini, bell pepper, gingerroot and garlic; stir-fry 1 minute. Stir in broth and 1 tablespoon soy sauce; heat to boiling. Stir in beef mixture. Mix cornstarch and cold water; stir into beef mixture. Cook and stir about 20 seconds or until thickened. Serve over rice.

| 1 Serving: | | | % Daily Value: | |
|---|---|---|---|---|
| Calories | 215 | | Vitamin A | 10% |
| Calories from fat | 35 | | Vitamin C | 26% |
| Fat, g | 4 | | Calcium | 4% |
| Saturated, g | 2 | | Iron | 16% |
| Cholesterol, mg | 30 | | **Diet Exchanges:** | |
| Sodium, mg | 430 | | Starch/bread | 2 |
| Carbohydrate, g | 31 | | Lean meat | 1 |
| Dietary Fiber, g | 2 | | | |
| Protein, g | 16 | | | |

# MONGOLIAN FIREPOT

**4** SERVINGS

*(photograph on page 119)*

*The Mongolian firepot is a centuries-old vessel heated by charcoal placed below a ring-shaped dish with a center chimney. However, modern electric appliances such as fondue pots or chafing dishes provide a much safer way to continue this fun tradition of communal eating. The firepot produces an almost complete low-fat meal—all you add is dessert. Once the pork and vegetables are cooked, you add spinach and noodles to the broth and serve as soup.*

**1 pound pork tenderloin**

**1 1/2 cups baby-cut carrots, cut lengthwise in half**

**3 cans (14 1/2 ounces each) fat-free reduced-sodium chicken broth**

**2 tablespoons purchased Sichuan sauce or Easy Sichuan Sauce (page 124)**

**1 cup small mushrooms, cut in half (6 ounces)**

**3 small zucchini, cut into 1-inch cubes**

**Choice of sauces, such as Hot Mustard Sauce (page 123), Lime Dipping Sauce (page 120), Orange-Ginger Sauce (page 122) or Sweet-and-Sour Plum Sauce (page 122)**

**4 cups hot cooked rice**

**2 ounces uncooked cellophane noodles (bean threads)**

**1 cup slightly packed shredded spinach leaves**

Trim fat from pork. Cut pork into 1/4-inch slices.

Heat broth and Sichuan sauce to boiling. Loosely roll up larger pork slices; leave smaller pieces flat. Pack pork, carrots, mushrooms and zucchini in 2-quart fondue pot or saucepan, alternating pork and vegetables. Gently pour boiling broth mixture into pot to cover pork and vegetables, add boiling water, if necessary. Heat to boiling; reduce heat to medium-low. Cover and simmer 20 to 30 minutes or until pork is no longer pink in center and carrots are tender. Prepare desired sauces.

To serve, place fondue pot over burner on table. Remove pork rolls and vegetable pieces with chopsticks or fondue forks, eating rice and sauces as accompaniments.

Meanwhile, soak cellophane noodles in boiling water 20 minutes; drain and chop into 2-inch pieces. When pot is empty of pork and vegetables, add noodles and spinach to broth. Cook 2 to 3 minutes or until spinach is wilted. Serve as soup.

| 1 Serving: | | % Daily Value: | |
|---|---|---|---|
| Calories | 475 | Vitamin A | 76% |
| Calories from fat | 115 | Vitamin C | 16% |
| Fat, g | 12 | Calcium | 6% |
| Saturated, g | 3 | Iron | 26% |
| Cholesterol, mg | 65 | **Diet Exchanges:** | |
| Sodium, mg | 800 | Starch/bread | 3 |
| Carbohydrate, g | 62 | Lean meat | 3 |
| Dietary Fiber, g | 4 | Fruit | 1 |
| Protein, g | 32 | | |

# BRAISED PORK TENDERLOIN IN RED SAUCE

**4** SERVINGS (6 SLICES EACH)

*Chinese red cooked meats are tender, flavorful and low in fat. This delicious, easy oven-baked recipe can be cooked for a crowd by simply increasing the amount of meat and using a larger pan—the baking time remains the same. The meat can be served either hot or cold.*

**1 pound pork tenderloin**

**1/4 cup water**

**2 tablespoons mushroom soy sauce**

**2 teaspoons seasoned rice vinegar**

**4 thin slices pickled ginger\* or fresh gingerroot**

**1 stick cinnamon**

**Green Onion Flowers (page 9)**

Heat oven to 450°. Spray 8-inch square pan with nonstick cooking spray. Trim fat from pork. Cut pork crosswise in half; place in pan. Roast uncovered 25 to 30 minutes or until brown.

Meanwhile heat water, soy sauce, vinegar, gingerroot and cinnamon to boiling in 1-quart saucepan; reduce heat to low. Simmer uncovered 20 minutes. Remove and discard cinnamon and ginger.

Pour soy sauce mixture over pork. Cover and bake 15 to 20 minutes, brushing with soy sauce mixture several times, until medium doneness (160°) or slightly pink in center. Meanwhile, prepare Green Onion Flowers. Remove pork from pan; place on cutting board. Reserve pan drippings if desired. Cover pork and let stand 10 minutes.

Cut pork into 1/4-inch slices; arrange on serving platter. Garnish with Green Onion Flowers. Serve with pan drippings if desired.

*\*Pickled Gingerroot (page 127) or purchased pickled ginger can be used.*

| 6 Slices: | | % Daily Value: | |
|---|---|---|---|
| Calories | 135 | Vitamin A | 0% |
| Calories from fat | 35 | Vitamin C | 0% |
| Fat, g | 4 | Calcium | 0% |
| Saturated, g | 1 | Iron | 8% |
| Cholesterol, mg | 65 | **Diet Exchanges:** | |
| Sodium, mg | 560 | Lean meat | 3 |
| Carbohydrate, g | 1 | | |
| Dietary Fiber, g | 0 | | |
| Protein, g | 24 | | |

*Braised Pork Tenderloin in Red Sauce, Stir-fried Green Beans with Sichuan Sauce (page 109)*

# SWEET-AND-SOUR PORK

### 6 SERVINGS

*We've cut 75 percent of the fat and half the sodium from this favorite recipe! The good news is you'll never miss it when you taste this rich sweet-and-sour sauce.*

**1 pound pork tenderloin**

**1 egg white, slightly beaten**

**1 teaspoon cornstarch**

**1 teaspoon soy sauce**

**1/4 teaspoon white pepper**

**1 teaspoon vegetable oil**

**1 medium green bell pepper, cut into 1-inch pieces**

**1/3 cup sugar**

**1 can (8 ounces) pineapple chunks in juice, drained and 1/2 cup juice reserved**

**2 tablespoons rice or white vinegar**

**2 tablespoons dark soy sauce**

**1 clove garlic, finely chopped**

**1 tablespoon cornstarch**

**1 tablespoon cold water**

**2 roma (plum) tomatoes, cut into eighths**

Trim fat from pork. Cut pork into 3/4-inch pieces. Mix egg white, 1 teaspoon cornstarch, 1 teaspoon soy sauce and the white pepper in medium glass or plastic bowl. Stir in pork. Let stand 10 minutes.

Spray nonstick wok or 12-inch skillet with cooking spray; heat over medium-high heat until cooking spray starts to bubble. Add oil; rotate wok to coat side. Add half of the pork; stir-fry 2 to 3 minutes or until no longer pink in center. Remove pork from wok. Repeat with remaining pork. Add bell pepper to wok; stir-fry about 2 minutes or until crisp-tender. Remove bell pepper from wok.

Heat sugar, reserved pineapple juice, the vinegar, dark soy sauce and garlic to boiling in wok over medium heat, stirring frequently. Mix 1 tablespoon cornstarch and the cold water; stir into sauce. Cook and stir about 20 seconds or until thickened. Stir in pork, bell pepper, pineapple and tomatoes. Cook and stir 1 minute or until heated through.

| 1 Serving: | | % Daily Value: | |
|---|---|---|---|
| Calories | 190 | Vitamin A | 4% |
| Calories from fat | 35 | Vitamin C | 18% |
| Fat, g | 4 | Calcium | 0% |
| Saturated, g | 1 | Iron | 6% |
| Cholesterol, mg | 45 | **Diet Exchanges:** | |
| Sodium, mg | 160 | Lean meat | 2 |
| Carbohydrate, g | 22 | Vegetable | 1 |
| Dietary Fiber, g | 1 | Fruit | 1 |
| Protein, g | 17 | | |

# SESAME PORK AND CARROT LO MEIN

**4** SERVINGS

*In this recipe just one teaspoon of sesame oil adds a unique flavor as well as preventing foods from sticking to the wok. If using regular bok choy instead of baby bok choy, do not use the stems.*

**1/2 pound pork tenderloin**

**1 egg white, slightly beaten**

**1 tablespoon cornstarch**

**1 teaspoon soy sauce**

**1/8 teaspoon white pepper**

**1 teaspoon sesame or vegetable oil**

**4 medium carrots, cut into 1/4-inch diagonal slices (2 cups)**

**1 package (about 7 ounces) fresh (refrigerated) lo mein noodles with teriyaki sauce***

**1 cup fat-free reduced-sodium chicken broth**

**1 head baby bok choy or leaves of regular bok choy, shredded (2 cups)**

**2 teaspoons sesame seed, toasted**

Trim fat from pork. Cut pork into 1/2-inch cubes. Mix egg white, cornstarch, soy sauce and white pepper in medium glass or plastic bowl. Stir in pork. Let stand 10 minutes.

Spray nonstick wok or 12-inch skillet with nonstick cooking spray; heat over medium-high heat until cooking spray starts to bubble. Add sesame oil; rotate wok to coat side. Add half of the pork; stir-fry 2 to 3 minutes or until no longer pink in center. Remove pork from wok. Repeat with remaining pork.

Add carrots to wok; stir-fry 2 minutes. Stir in noodles, contents of sauce packet and broth. Stir noodles to separate; return pork to wok. Cover and cook 1 to 2 minutes or until carrots are crisp-tender. Add bok-choy; stir-fry about 1 minute or until wilted. Sprinkle with sesame seed.

*4 ounces thin spaghetti, cooked, and 1/4 cup purchased teriyaki sauce can be substituted for the lo mein noodles with sauce.

| 1 Serving: | | % Daily Value: | |
|---|---|---|---|
| Calories | 235 | Vitamin A | 100% |
| Calories from fat | 45 | Vitamin C | 18% |
| Fat, g | 5 | Calcium | 6% |
| Saturated, g | 1 | Iron | 8% |
| Cholesterol, mg | 35 | **Diet Exchanges:** | |
| Sodium, mg | 620 | Starch/bread | 2 |
| Carbohydrate, g | 33 | Lean meat | 1 |
| Dietary Fiber, g | 3 | Vegetable | 1 |
| Protein, g | 18 | | |

# CRISPY PORK WITH SWEET-AND-SOUR VEGETABLES

**4** SERVINGS

*Rice cracker crumbs are used in place of the traditional deep-fried batter coating to create a low-fat crisp-crumb coating. Using a skillet rather than a wok allows for all of the pork to come in contact with the surface of the pan so it browns evenly. It's best to brown the meat with a minimum of turning.*

**1/2 pound pork tenderloin**

**1 egg white, slightly beaten**

**1 teaspoon water**

**24 crisp rice crackers, crushed (1/2 cup)**

**1/4 teaspoon garlic powder**

**1/4 teaspoon ground mustard (dry)**

**1 teaspoon sesame or vegetable oil**

**1 package (1 pound 5 ounces) frozen stir-fry vegetables with sweet-and-sour sauce and pineapple***

Trim fat from pork. Cut pork crosswise into 1/4-inch slices; stack slices and cut lengthwise into 1/2-inch strips. Mix egg white and water in medium bowl. Stir in pork until well coated.

Mix crushed crackers, garlic powder and mustard in plastic bag or glass bowl. Add a few pork strips at a time; toss to coat evenly.

Spray 12-inch nonstick skillet with nonstick cooking spray; heat over medium-high heat until cooking spray starts to bubble. Add sesame oil; rotate skillet to coat bottom. Reduce heat to medium. Place pork strips flat in skillet; cook 2 to 3 minutes or until brown on bottom. Turn pork. Cook 2 to 3 minutes longer or until no longer pink in center. Remove pork from skillet.

Wipe skillet clean. Add frozen vegetables and sauce. Cover and cook 7 to 10 minutes, stirring frequently, until vegetables are crisp-tender and sauce is hot. Gently stir in pork strips just until well coated with sauce. Serve immediately.

*Frozen stir-fry vegetables without sauce and 1/2 cup purchased sweet-and-sour sauce can be substituted for the vegetables with sauce.

| 1 Serving: | | % Daily Value: | |
|---|---|---|---|
| Calories | 240 | Vitamin A | 14% |
| Calories from fat | 55 | Vitamin C | 30% |
| Fat, g | 6 | Calcium | 4% |
| Saturated, g | 2 | Iron | 12% |
| Cholesterol, mg | 35 | **Diet Exchanges:** | |
| Sodium, mg | 710 | Starch/bread | 1 |
| Carbohydrate, g | 33 | Lean meat | 1 |
| Dietary Fiber, g | 4 | Vegetable | 1 |
| Protein, g | 17 | Fruit | 1 |

*Crispy Pork with Sweet-and-Sour Vegetables*

# ❤ LEMON BROCCOLI PORK

### 4 SERVINGS

*When time allows, marinate the pork overnight. With the enhanced flavor you'll never miss the stir-fry oil.*

**Lemon Dipping Sauce (page 120)**

**1/2 pound pork tenderloin**

**1/2 cup fat-free reduced-sodium chicken broth**

**1 teaspoon finely chopped gingerroot**

**1 pound broccoli, cut into flowerets and 2 × 1/2-inch pieces (4 cups)**

**2 cups hot cooked rosamarina (orzo) pasta or rice**

**1 teaspoon finely shredded lemon peel**

Prepare Lemon Dipping Sauce in medium glass or plastic bowl. Trim fat from pork. Cut pork into 1/2-inch cubes; stir into sauce. Let stand 10 minutes, or cover and refrigerate no longer than 24 hours.

Drain pork; reserve sauce. Spray nonstick wok or 12-inch skillet with nonstick cooking spray; heat over medium-high heat until cooking spray starts to bubble. Add pork; stir-fry about 3 minutes or until no longer pink in center. Remove pork from wok.

Add broth and gingerroot to wok; heat to boiling. Add broccoli; stir-fry 1 minute over medium heat. Cover and cook about 3 minutes, stirring occasionally, until broccoli is crisp-tender. Add reserved sauce and the pork; cook and stir until well coated. Serve over pasta. Sprinkle with lemon peel.

| 1 Serving: | | % Daily Value: | |
|---|---|---|---|
| Calories | 185 | Vitamin A | 2% |
| Calories from fat | 25 | Vitamin C | 14% |
| Fat, g | 3 | Calcium | 2% |
| Saturated, g | 1 | Iron | 12% |
| Cholesterol, mg | 35 | **Diet Exchanges:** | |
| Sodium, mg | 860 | Starch/bread | 1 |
| Carbohydrate, g | 23 | Lean meat | 2 |
| Dietary Fiber, g | 1 | Vegetable | 1 |
| Protein, g | 17 | | |

# STIR-FRY PORK WITH BELL PEPPERS

**4** SERVINGS

*We've captured the flavor of Chinese spareribs in this dish by using lean pork tenderloin and fresh bell peppers as a lower-fat alternatives.*

**3/4 pound pork tenderloin**

**2 teaspoons cornstarch**

**2 teaspoons soy sauce**

**1 teaspoon sugar**

**2 green onions, cut into 2-inch pieces**

**1 tablespoon cold water**

**2 teaspoons cornstarch**

**1 teaspoon sugar**

**1/2 cup fat-free reduced-sodium chicken broth**

**1 teaspoon vegetable oil**

**1 tablespoon brown bean sauce**

**2 cloves garlic, finely chopped**

**1 teaspoon finely chopped gingerroot**

**2 green or red bell peppers, cut into 1-inch pieces**

Trim fat from pork. Cut pork lengthwise in half. Cut lengths crosswise into 1/4-inch slices. Mix 2 teaspoons cornstarch, the soy sauce and 1 teaspoon sugar in medium glass or plastic bowl. Stir in pork. Let stand 10 minutes. Cut green onion pieces into thin slices.

Mix cold water, 2 teaspoons cornstarch and 1 teaspoon sugar; stir in broth. Spray nonstick wok or 12-inch skillet with nonstick cooking spray; heat over medium-high heat until cooking spray starts to bubble. Add oil; rotate wok to coat side. Add half of the pork; stir-fry 2 to 3 minutes or until no longer pink in center. Remove pork from wok. Repeat with remaining pork. Return pork to wok.

Add bean sauce, garlic and gingerroot; stir-fry 1 minute. Pour cornstarch mixture into wok; cook and stir about 1 minute or until thickened. Add bell peppers; cook and stir 2 minutes or until crisp-tender. Sprinkle with green onion.

| 1 Serving: | | % Daily Value: | |
|---|---|---|---|
| Calories | 145 | Vitamin A | 2% |
| Calories from fat | 35 | Vitamin C | 28% |
| Fat, g | 4 | Calcium | 2% |
| Saturated, g | 1 | Iron | 8% |
| Cholesterol, mg | 50 | **Diet Exchanges:** | |
| Sodium, mg | 300 | Lean meat | 2 |
| Carbohydrate, g | 9 | Vegetable | 2 |
| Dietary Fiber, g | 1 | | |
| Protein, g | 19 | | |

# MOU SHU PORK

### 4 SERVINGS (2 POCKETS EACH)

*This classic favorite gets a healthy boost with the addition of Chinese cabbage. To make Mandarin Pancakes ahead, after folding each pancake into fourths, cover and refrigerate no longer than forty-eight hours or wrap, label and freeze no longer than two months. For a quick meal, use fat-free flour tortillas in place of homemade Mandarin Pancakes.*

**Mandarin Pancakes (recipe follows)**

**4 Green Onion Brushes (page 9), if desired**

**6 dried black (shiitake) mushrooms**

**1 can (8 ounces) sliced bamboo shoots, drained**

**3 pork boneless loin chops, 1/4 inch thick (1/2 pound)**

**1 teaspoon cornstarch**

**1 teaspoon soy sauce**

**1/2 teaspoon salt**

**1/2 teaspoon sugar**

**1/8 teaspoon white pepper**

**1/4 cup fat-free cholesterol-free egg product or 2 egg whites**

**1/8 teaspoon white pepper**

**1 teaspoon vegetable oil**

**3 stalks Chinese (napa) cabbage, shredded (1 1/2 cups)**

**2 cloves garlic, finely chopped**

**1 teaspoon soy sauce**

**2 green onions, chopped**

**8 teaspoons hoisin sauce**

Prepare Mandarin Pancakes and Green Onion Brushes. Soak mushrooms in hot water about 20 minutes or until soft; drain. Rinse with warm water; drain. Squeeze out excess moisture. Remove and discard stems; cut caps into thin strips. Cut bamboo shoots into thin strips.

Trim fat from pork. Cut pork lengthwise in half. Stack pork slices; cut diagonally into 1/4-inch strips. Mix cornstarch, 1 teaspoon soy sauce, the salt, sugar and 1/8 teaspoon white pepper in medium bowl. Stir in pork; let stand 10 min.

Mix egg product and 1/8 teaspoon white pepper. Spray nonstick wok or 12-inch skillet with non-stick cooking spray; heat over medium-high heat until cooking spray starts to bubble. Add egg mixture; rotate wok to coat bottom with egg, forming a thin layer. Cook 10 to 30 seconds, turning once, until set. Remove egg from wok. Cool slightly; cut into thin strips.

Cool wok slightly. Wipe clean and respray. Add oil and rotate wok to coat side. Heat over medium-high heat. Add pork; stir-fry about 2 minutes or until no longer pink in center. Add mushrooms, bamboo shoots, cabbage, garlic, 1 teaspoon soy sauce and the green onions; stir-fry about 1 minute or until cabbage is wilted. Gently stir in egg strips.

To serve, brush 1 teaspoon hoisin sauce on each pancake with onion brush. Spoon 1/4 cup pork mixture onto center of pancake. Fold 2 opposite sides over filling, overlapping edges about 1/2 inch in center. Fold 1 unfolded side over folded sides to form a pocket. Or serve hoisin sauce as a dip.

*1. Brush circle with sesame oil; top with another circle.*

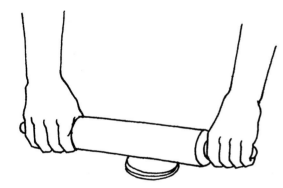

*2. Roll double circle into a 7-inch circle.*

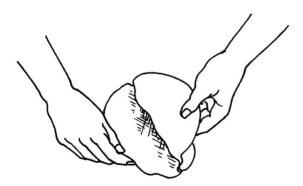

*3. After frying, carefully separate into 2 pancakes; fold each pancake loosely into fourths.*

## MANDARIN PANCAKES

**1 cup plus 2 tablespoons all-purpose flour**
**1/2 cup boiling water**
**Sesame oil**

Mix flour and water with fork until dough forms. Turn dough onto lightly floured surface. Knead about 8 minutes or until smooth. Shape dough into 4-inch roll; cut roll into four 1-inch slices. Cut each slice in half. (Cover pieces of dough with plastic wrap to keep them from drying out.)

Shape 2 pieces of dough into balls. Flatten each ball of dough slightly and roll into 4-inch circles on lightly floured surface. Brush top of one circle with sesame oil; top with remaining circle. Roll each double circle into 7-inch circle. Repeat with remaining pieces of dough. (Cover circles with plastic wrap to keep them from drying out.)

Heat ungreased 8- or 9-inch nonstick skillet over medium heat until warm. Cook one double circle at a time, turning frequently, until pancake is blistered with air pockets, turns slightly translucent and feels dry. (Do not overcook or pancake will become brittle.) Carefully separate into 2 pancakes; fold each pancake into fourths. Repeat each step with remaining circles.

Heat pancakes before serving: Place folded pancakes on heatproof plate or rack in steamer. Cover and steam over boiling water in wok or Dutch oven 10 minutes, adding boiling water if necessary. Or, place folded pancake on microwavable plate. Cover with dampened microwavable paper towel or microwave plastic wrap and microwave on High (100 percent power) for 20 to 30 seconds.

| 2 Pockets: | | % Daily Value: | |
|---|---|---|---|
| Calories | 295 | Vitamin A | 6% |
| Calories from fat | 80 | Vitamin C | 12% |
| Fat, g | 9 | Calcium | 6% |
| Saturated, g | 2 | Iron | 18% |
| Cholesterol, mg | 35 | **Diet Exchanges:** | |
| Sodium, mg | 490 | Starch/bread | 2 |
| Carbohydrate, g | 37 | Lean meat | 2 |
| Dietary Fiber, g | 3 | Vegetable | 1 |
| Protein, g | 20 | | |

# ORANGE-GINGER PORK WITH VEGETABLES

### **4** SERVINGS

*No other cut of pork is lower in fat grams than the flavorful tenderloin, and it's put to good use in this satisfying stir-fry.*

**1/4 cup Orange-Ginger Sauce (page 122)**

**1/2 pound pork tenderloin**

**1 teaspoon soy sauce**

**1 package (16 ounces) frozen broccoli, carrots and water chestnuts**

**2 cups hot cooked rice**

Prepare Orange-Ginger Sauce. Trim fat from pork. Cut pork into 1/8-inch slices.

Spray nonstick wok or 12-inch skillet with nonstick cooking spray; heat over medium-high heat until cooking spray starts to bubble. Add pork; stir-fry 2 to 3 minutes or until no longer pink in center. Add Orange-Ginger Sauce and soy sauce; stir until pork is coated. Heat to boiling.

Gently stir in vegetables until well coated; reduce heat to medium. Cover and cook about 5 minutes, stirring frequently, until vegetables are hot. Serve over rice.

| 1 Serving: | | % Daily Value: | |
|---|---|---|---|
| Calories | 240 | Vitamin A | 78% |
| Calories from fat | 55 | Vitamin C | 28% |
| Fat, g | 6 | Calcium | 4% |
| Saturated, g | 2 | Iron | 12% |
| Cholesterol, mg | 35 | **Diet Exchanges:** | |
| Sodium, mg | 145 | Starch/bread | 2 |
| Carbohydrate, g | 33 | Lean meat | 1 |
| Dietary Fiber, g | 3 | Vegetable | 1 |
| Protein, g | 16 | | |

# ♥ EASY CANTON PORK WITH TOMATOES

### **4** SERVINGS

*Frozen precut vegetables with their own sauce make this a quick family main dish, welcome after a busy day.*

**1/2 pound pork tenderloin**

**1 package (1 pound 5 ounces) frozen stir-fry vegetables with Cantonese sauce and almonds**

**3 medium roma (plum) tomatoes, cut into eighths**

Trim fat from pork. Cut pork crosswise into 1/4-inch slices; stack slices and cut crosswise into 1/4-inch sticks.

Spray nonstick wok or 12-inch skillet with nonstick cooking spray; heat over medium-high heat until cooking spray starts to bubble. Add pork; stir-fry 2 to 3 minutes or until no longer pink in center. Add frozen vegetables and sauce. Cover and cook 7 to 10 minutes, stirring frequently, until vegetables are crisp-tender. Add tomatoes and almonds; stir to coat evenly with sauce.

| 1 Serving: | | % Daily Value: | |
|---|---|---|---|
| Calories | 155 | Vitamin A | 6% |
| Calories from fat | 20 | Vitamin C | 14% |
| Fat, g | 2 | Calcium | 0% |
| Saturated, g | 1 | Iron | 6% |
| Cholesterol, mg | 35 | **Diet Exchanges:** | |
| Sodium, mg | 280 | Starch/bread | 1 |
| Carbohydrate, g | 22 | Lean meat | 1 |
| Dietary Fiber, g | 3 | Vegetable | 1 |
| Protein, g | 15 | | |

*Easy Canton Pork with Tomatoes, Coconut-Ginger Rice (page 103)*

# 5

# RICE, NOODLES AND VEGETABLES

*Oven-Fried Rice (page 102)*

# OVEN-FRIED RICE

### 6 SERVINGS

*(photograph on page 101)*

*We baked cooked rice before stir-frying with egg and vegetables to eliminate the fat and calories typical of fried rice. This recipe is also a great way to use leftover rice and meat.*

**1 tablespoon vegetable oil**

**3 cups cooked white rice**

**1 teaspoon vegetable oil**

**3/4 cup fat-free cholesterol-free egg product or 6 egg whites, slightly beaten**

**1 teaspoon vegetable oil**

**1 package (8 ounces) fresh bean sprouts or 1 can (14 to 16 ounces) bean sprouts, rinsed and drained**

**1 can (7 ounces) button mushrooms, drained**

**1/2 cup chopped cooked Barbecued Pork (page 14) or other meat, if desired**

**2 tablespoons dark soy sauce**

**1/2 teaspoon salt**

**Dash of white pepper**

**1/2 cup frozen green peas, thawed**

**1/4 cup chopped green onions (3 medium)**

Heat oven to 425°. Line cookie sheet with aluminum foil; spray with nonstick cooking spray. Stir 1 tablespoon oil into rice. Spread rice evenly on foil. Bake 30 to 35 minutes, stirring several times, until brown and crisp.

Spray nonstick wok or 12-inch skillet with nonstick cooking spray; heat over medium-high heat until cooking spray starts to bubble. Add 1 teaspoon oil; rotate wok to coat side. Add egg product; cook and stir about 30 seconds or until eggs are thickened throughout but still moist. Remove eggs from wok; chop coarsely.

Mix soy sauce, salt and white pepper. Cool wok slightly; wipe clean. Add 1 teaspoon oil; rotate wok to coat side. Heat over medium-high heat. Add bean sprouts and mushrooms; stir-fry 1 minute. Stir in rice and Barbecued Pork. Add soy-sauce mixture, peas, green onions and eggs; stir-fry 30 seconds.

| 1 Serving: | | % Daily Value: | |
|---|---|---|---|
| Calories | 215 | Vitamin A | 2% |
| Calories from fat | 65 | Vitamin C | 6% |
| Fat, g | 7 | Calcium | 4% |
| Saturated, g | 1 | Iron | 16% |
| Cholesterol, mg | 0 | **Diet Exchanges:** | |
| Sodium, mg | 650 | Starch/bread | 2 |
| Carbohydrate, g | 30 | Lean meat | 1 |
| Dietary Fiber, g | 3 | | |
| Protein, g | 11 | | |

# STIR-FRIED LEMON RICE WITH SPINACH

### 4 SERVINGS

*Rice and vegetables combine to make this a tangy side or a light lemony main dish meal for two.*

**2 green onions**

**2 tablespoons soy sauce**

**2 tablespoons lemon juice**

**2 teaspoons grated gingerroot**

**1 teaspoon grated lemon peel**

**1 clove garlic, finely chopped**

**1 medium yellow summer squash, cut into
    1/4-inch slices (2 cups)**

**1 teaspoon sesame oil**

**2 cups shredded spinach (3 ounces)**

**2 cups cooked white rice**

Cut green onions into 2-inch pieces; cut pieces lengthwise into thin slices. Mix soy sauce, lemon juice, gingerroot, lemon peel and garlic; toss with squash and green onions. Cover and let stand 15 minutes.

Spray nonstick wok or 12-inch skillet with non-stick cooking spray; heat over medium-high heat until cooking spray starts to bubble. Add sesame oil; rotate wok to coat side. Add spinach; stir-fry 15 seconds. Add squash mixture; stir-fry 1 minute. Add rice; stir-fry about 1 minute or until heated through.

| 1 Serving: | | % Daily Value: | |
| --- | --- | --- | --- |
| Calories | 140 | Vitamin A | 20% |
| Calories from fat | 20 | Vitamin C | 12% |
| Fat, g | 2 | Calcium | 4% |
| Saturated, g | 0 | Iron | 10% |
| Cholesterol, mg | 0 | **Diet Exchanges:** | |
| Sodium, mg | 540 | Starch/bread | 1 1/2 |
| Carbohydrate, g | 27 | Vegetable | 1 |
| Dietary Fiber, g | 1 | | |
| Protein, g | 4 | | |

# COCONUT-GINGER RICE

### 6 SERVINGS (1/2 CUP EACH)

*Buy reduced-fat coconut milk for the same creamy rich taste but with only half the fat of regular coconut milk.*

**1 can (14 1/2 ounces) fat-free reduced-
    sodium chicken broth**

**1/2 cup reduced-fat (lite) coconut milk**

**2 teaspoons grated gingerroot**

**1/2 teaspoon salt**

**1 cup uncooked regular long grain rice**

**1/2 teaspoon grated lime peel**

**2 green onions, chopped**

**2 tablespoons flaked coconut, toasted***

**Lime slices**

Heat broth, coconut milk, gingerroot and salt to boiling in 2-quart saucepan over medium-high heat. Stir in rice. Heat to boiling; reduce heat. Cover and simmer 14 to 16 minutes (do not lift cover or stir) or until rice is tender and liquid is absorbed.

Add lime peel and green onions; fluff rice, lime peel and green onions lightly with fork to mix. Garnish with coconut and lime slices.

*To toast coconut, heat oven to 300°. Spread coconut evenly on ungreased cookie sheet. Bake about 10 minutes, stirring occasionally, until golden brown.

| 1 Serving: | | % Daily Value: | |
| --- | --- | --- | --- |
| Calories | 135 | Vitamin A | 0% |
| Calories from fat | 20 | Vitamin C | 0% |
| Fat, g | 2 | Calcium | 2% |
| Saturated, g | 1 | Iron | 10% |
| Cholesterol, mg | 0 | **Diet Exchanges:** | |
| Sodium, mg | 310 | Starch/bread | 1 |
| Carbohydrate, g | 27 | Fruit | 1 |
| Dietary Fiber, g | 1 | | |
| Protein, g | 3 | | |

# RICE EGG FOO YUNG

## 4 SERVINGS

*Egg Foo Yung is an Oriental omelet. This low-fat, meatless entrée makes a quick, light meal.*

**Egg Foo Yung Sauce (right)**

**1 teaspoon vegetable oil**

**1 cup coarsely chopped bean sprouts (1 ounce)**

**1/3 cup chopped red bell pepper**

**1/4 cup chopped celery***

**2 cloves garlic, finely chopped**

**3/4 cup cooked white or brown rice**

**1 1/2 containers (8-ounce size) fat-free cholesterol-free egg product (1 1/2 cups) or 9 egg whites**

**1/2 teaspoon salt**

**2 teaspoons vegetable oil**

Prepare Egg Foo Yung Sauce. Spray nonstick wok or 12-inch skillet with nonstick cooking spray; heat over medium-high heat until cooking spray starts to bubble. Add 1 teaspoon oil; rotate wok to coat side. Add bean sprouts, bell pepper, celery, cashews and garlic; stir-fry 1 minute. Add rice; stir-fry 1 minute. Remove rice mixture from skillet; cool skillet. Mix egg product and salt.

Wipe skillet clean. Respray and add 1 teaspoon oil; rotate skillet to coat bottom. Heat over medium-high heat. Add half of the rice mixture; spread evenly in skillet. Pour half of the egg mixture over rice. As mixture begins to set at bottom and side,

gently lift cooked portions with spatula so that thin, uncooked portion can flow to bottom. Cook about 2 minutes or until bottom is light brown. Cut in half or fourths with end of spatula; turn over. Cook 2 minutes longer. Remove omelet from skillet and keep warm. Repeat with remaining oil, rice mixture and egg mixture. Top with Egg Foo Yung Sauce. Garnish with celery leaves if desired.

*Celery leaves can be reserved for garnish.

### EGG FOO YUNG SAUCE

**1/2 cup fat-free reduced-sodium chicken broth**

**1 tablespoon dark soy sauce**

**2 teaspoons cornstarch**

**2 teaspoons cold water**

Heat broth and soy sauce to boiling in 1-quart saucepan. Mix cornstarch and cold water; stir into broth mixture. Cook and stir about 1 minute or until thickened.

| 1 Serving: | | % Daily Value: | |
|---|---|---|---|
| Calories | 140 | Vitamin A | 8% |
| Calories from fat | 45 | Vitamin C | 16% |
| Fat, g | 5 | Calcium | 4% |
| Saturated, g | 1 | Iron | 14% |
| Cholesterol, mg | 0 | **Diet Exchanges:** | |
| Sodium, mg | 710 | Starch/bread | 1 |
| Carbohydrate, g | 15 | Lean meat | 1 |
| Dietary Fiber, g | 2 | | |
| Protein, g | 11 | | |

# EASY TWO-PAN LO MEIN

**4** SERVINGS

*This simplified two-pan method reduces the fat in the recipe and also makes it easy to substitute other vegetables and cooked meats. Cook any dense vegetables in the noodle water; stir-fry less dense vegetables and cooked meat in the wok. Then, toss it all in the stir-fry sauce.*

**4 stalks Chinese (napa) cabbage (8 ounces)**

**2 quarts water**

**12 baby-cut carrots, cut lengthwise into 1/4-inch sticks (1 1/2 cups)**

**6 ounces dried Chinese noodles**

**Garlic Stir-fry Sauce (page 124)**

**1 teaspoon vegetable oil**

**1 cup sliced mushrooms (3 ounces)**

**1/2 cup sliced Barbecued Pork (page 14), cut into 1/4-inch sticks***

Separate cabbage leaves from stems. Cut leaves into 2-inch pieces; cut stems into 1/4-inch diagonal slices (do not combine leaves and stems). Heat 2 quarts water to boiling in Dutch oven. Stir in cabbage stems, carrots and noodles, breaking noodles into 3-inch pieces. Cook uncovered over medium heat about 5 minutes or until noodles are tender and can be separated; drain.

Prepare Garlic Stir-fry Sauce—except do not cook. Spray nonstick wok or 12-inch skillet with nonstick cooking spray; heat over medium-high heat until cooking spray starts to bubble. Add oil; rotate wok to coat side. Add cabbage leaves and mushrooms; stir-fry 1 minute. Add stir-fry sauce; cook and stir about 1 minute or until thickened. Add Barbecued Pork and noodle mixture; reduce heat to low. Cook and stir until heated through.

*1/2 cup chopped cooked shrimp can be substituted for the pork; add 1 tablespoon oyster sauce to the Garlic Stir-fry Sauce before adding to the wok.

| 1 Serving: | | % Daily Value: | |
|---|---|---|---|
| Calories | 185 | Vitamin A | 78% |
| Calories from fat | 25 | Vitamin C | 16% |
| Fat, g | 3 | Calcium | 6% |
| Saturated, g | 1 | Iron | 8% |
| Cholesterol, mg | 15 | **Diet Exchanges:** | |
| Sodium, mg | 420 | Starch/bread | 2 |
| Carbohydrate, g | 35 | Vegetable | 1 |
| Dietary Fiber, g | 3 | | |
| Protein, g | 8 | | |

# NOODLE PANCAKES WITH PEANUT SAUCE

**4** SERVINGS

**Warm Peanut Dressing (page 126)**

**1 package (8 ounces) dried thin Chinese noodles or 8 ounces uncooked angel hair pasta**

**2 teaspoons vegetable oil**

**1 medium green bell pepper, cut into 2 × 1/4-inch strips**

**3 green onions, chopped**

**1 small red jalapeño chile, seeded and finely chopped**

Prepare Warm Peanut Dressing as directed—except increase cornstarch to 1 tablespoon. Cook and drain noodles as directed on package—except break noodles into 3-inch pieces before cooking. Do not rinse noodles.

Heat oven to 250°. Spray 12-inch nonstick skillet with nonstick cooking spray; heat over medium-low heat until cooking spray starts to bubble. Add 1 teaspoon of the oil; rotate skillet to coat bottom. Add half of the noodles, spreading into flat circle. Cook 8 to 10 minutes or until bottom is crisp and brown on bottom. Turn pancake upside down onto flat plate. Slide uncooked side into skillet. Cook 8 to 10 minutes or until surface is crisp but center is tender. Keep warm on cookie sheet in oven. Repeat with remaining oil and noodles.

Cool skillet slightly. Wipe clean; respray and heat over medium-high heat until cooking spray starts to bubble. Add bell pepper, green onions and chile; stir-fry 1 minute. Stir in 1/4 cup of the peanut sauce; heat through. Spoon mixture on top of pancake. Cut each pancake in half. Serve with remaining peanut sauce.

| 1 Serving: | | % Daily Value: | |
|---|---|---|---|
| Calories | 220 | Vitamin A | 12% |
| Calories from fat | 55 | Vitamin C | 36% |
| Fat, g | 6 | Calcium | 2% |
| Saturated, g | 1 | Iron | 8% |
| Cholesterol, mg | 0 | **Diet Exchanges:** | |
| Sodium, mg | 210 | Starch/bread | 2 |
| Carbohydrate, g | 40 | Vegetable | 2 |
| Dietary Fiber, g | 2 | | |
| Protein, g | 4 | | |

*Noodle Pancakes with Peanut Sauce*

# HOT-AND-SOUR CABBAGE

### 4 SERVINGS

**2 teaspoons vegetable oil**

**1 small head cabbage (1 pound), cut into 1 1/2-inch pieces**

**1/4 cup ketchup**

**1 teaspoon salt**

**1 teaspoon red pepper sauce**

**2 large cloves garlic, finely chopped**

**1/2 cup fat-free reduced-sodium chicken broth**

**1 tablespoon cornstarch**

**1 tablespoon cold water**

**1/2 cup crunchy toasted corn kernel nuts, if desired**

**3 green onions, cut into 2 × 1/8-inch strips**

Spray nonstick wok or 12-inch skillet with non-stick cooking spray; heat over medium-high heat until cooking spray starts to bubble. Add oil; rotate wok to coat side. Add cabbage; stir-fry 1 minute. Add ketchup, salt, pepper sauce and garlic; stir-fry 1 minute.

Stir in broth; heat to boiling. Mix cornstarch and cold water; stir into cabbage mixture. Cook and stir about 10 seconds or until thickened. Stir in corn nuts and green onions.

| 1 Serving: | | % Daily Value: | |
|---|---|---|---|
| Calories | 90 | Vitamin A | 4% |
| Calories from fat | 25 | Vitamin C | 52% |
| Fat, g | 3 | Calcium | 10% |
| Saturated, g | 1 | Iron | 8% |
| Cholesterol, mg | 0 | **Diet Exchanges:** | |
| Sodium, mg | 810 | Starch/bread | 1/2 |
| Carbohydrate, g | 17 | Vegetable | 1 |
| Dietary Fiber, g | 4 | | |
| Protein, g | 3 | | |

# ORANGE-GINGER CAULIFLOWER AND CARROTS

### 4 SERVINGS

**1/4 cup Orange-Ginger Sauce (page 122)**

**1 teaspoon cornstarch**

**1 small head cauliflower (1 1/2 pounds), cut into flowerets (3 cups)**

**3 medium carrots, cut into 1/4-inch diagonal slices (1 1/2 cups)**

**2 green onions, chopped**

**Orange sections, if desired***

Prepare Orange-Ginger Sauce. Mix cornstarch and small amount of sauce until smooth; stir into remaining sauce.

Cook cauliflower and carrots in boiling water 2 minutes; drain. Immediately rinse with cold water; drain.

Spray nonstick wok or 12-inch skillet with non-stick cooking spray; heat over medium-high heat until cooking spray starts to bubble. Add cauli-flower and carrots; stir-fry 1 minute. Stir sauce; stir into cauliflower mixture. Cook and stir about 1 minute until sauce is thickened. Stir in green onions and orange sections.

*Reserve half of the orange when making Orange-Ginger Sauce; separate into sections.*

| 1 Serving: | | % Daily Value: | |
|---|---|---|---|
| Calories | 85 | Vitamin A | 78% |
| Calories from fat | 35 | Vitamin C | 32% |
| Fat, g | 4 | Calcium | 4% |
| Saturated, g | 1 | Iron | 4% |
| Cholesterol, mg | 0 | **Diet Exchanges:** | |
| Sodium, mg | 40 | Vegetable | 2 |
| Carbohydrate, g | 13 | Fat | 1 |
| Dietary Fiber, g | 3 | | |
| Protein, g | 2 | | |

# STIR-FRY ASPARAGUS WITH SICHUAN SAUCE

### 4 SERVINGS

**2 teaspoons sesame seed**

**1 teaspoon sugar**

**1 teaspoon sesame oil**

**1 teaspoon chile puree with garlic**

**1 pound asparagus, cut into 2-inch diagonal pieces**

**1/4 cup fat-free reduced-sodium chicken broth**

Heat nonstick wok or 12-inch skillet over medium-high heat until hot; reduce heat to medium-low. Add sesame seed; cook and stir about 2 minutes or until light brown. Remove sesame seed from wok.

Mix sugar, sesame oil and chile puree. Cool wok slightly; wipe clean. Spray with nonstick cooking spray and heat over medium-high heat until cooking spray starts to bubble. Add asparagus; stir-fry 1 minute. Stir in broth; cover and cook 2 minutes. Add chile sauce mixture; stir-fry 1 minute. Stir in sesame seed.

| 1 Serving: | | % Daily Value: | |
|---|---|---|---|
| Calories | 40 | Vitamin A | 4% |
| Calories from fat | 20 | Vitamin C | 10% |
| Fat, g | 2 | Calcium | 2% |
| Saturated, g | 0 | Iron | 2% |
| Cholesterol, mg | 0 | **Diet Exchanges:** | |
| Sodium, mg | 45 | Vegetable | 1 |
| Carbohydrate, g | 4 | | |
| Dietary Fiber, g | 1 | | |
| Protein, g | 2 | | |

# STIR-FRIED GREEN BEANS WITH SICHUAN SAUCE

### 4 SERVINGS

*(photograph on page 88)*

**1 tablespoon soy sauce**

**1 teaspoon sugar**

**1 teaspoon sesame oil**

**1 tablespoon chile puree with garlic**

**2 teaspoons cornstarch**

**2 teaspoons cold water**

**1 pound green beans, cut into 2-inch pieces (4 cups)**

**3/4 cup fat-free reduced-sodium chicken broth**

**1 teaspoon toasted sesame seed**

Mix soy sauce, sugar, sesame oil and chile puree. Mix cornstarch and cold water.

Spray nonstick wok or 12-inch skillet with nonstick cooking spray; heat over medium-high heat until cooking spray starts to bubble. Add green beans; stir-fry 1 to 2 minutes or until beans are bright green. Stir in broth; cover and cook over low heat 5 minutes.

Add soy sauce mixture and cornstarch mixture; stir-fry over high heat until beans are coated and sauce is thickened. Stir in sesame seed.

| 1 Serving: | | % Daily Value: | |
|---|---|---|---|
| Calories | 55 | Vitamin A | 4% |
| Calories from fat | 20 | Vitamin C | 6% |
| Fat, g | 2 | Calcium | 4% |
| Saturated, g | 0 | Iron | 4% |
| Cholesterol, mg | 0 | **Diet Exchanges:** | |
| Sodium, mg | 400 | Vegetable | 2 |
| Carbohydrate, g | 10 | | |
| Dietary Fiber, g | 3 | | |
| Protein, g | 2 | | |

# SWEET-AND-SOUR BROCCOLI AND BABY CORN

### 4 SERVINGS

*A tasty sweet-and-sour sauce with minimal cooking makes this broccoli dish delicious without any added fat. Leftover canned broth can be frozen in ice cube trays; remove when frozen and seal in freeze bag; one cube is about 1 tablespoon of broth.*

**1 pound broccoli, cut into flowerets and
    1-inch pieces (4 cups)**

**2 teaspoons cornstarch**

**2 teaspoons cold water**

**2 tablespoons fat-free reduced-sodium
    chicken broth**

**2 tablespoons honey**

**2 tablespoons lemon juice**

**1 tablespoon ketchup**

**1 teaspoon finely chopped garlic**

**1 teaspoon grated lemon peel**

**1/4 teaspoon salt**

**Dash of crushed red pepper, if desired**

**1 cup canned baby corn, rinsed and drained**

Cut any broccoli stems more than 1 inch wide lengthwise in half. Place broccoli in boiling water; heat to boiling. Boil 1 minute; drain. Immediately rinse with cold water; drain.

Mix cornstarch and cold water. Heat broth, honey, lemon juice, ketchup, garlic, lemon peel and salt to boiling in nonstick wok or 12-inch skillet, stirring frequently. Stir in cornstarch mixture. Cook and stir about 1 minute or until thickened.

Stir in red pepper. Add broccoli and corn; cook and stir about 30 seconds or until heated through.

*1 package (16 ounces) frozen broccoli cuts, thawed and drained, can be substituted for the fresh broccoli. Do not cook.

| 1 Serving: | | % Daily Value: | |
|---|---|---|---|
| Calories | 85 | Vitamin A | 10% |
| Calories from fat | 0 | Vitamin C | 56% |
| Fat, g | 0 | Calcium | 4% |
|   Saturated, g | 0 | Iron | 4% |
| Cholesterol, mg | 0 | **Diet Exchanges:** | |
| Sodium, mg | 210 | Vegetable | 1 |
| Carbohydrate, g | 21 | Fruit | 1 |
|   Dietary Fiber, g | 3 | | |
| Protein, g | 3 | | |

*Sweet-and-Sour Broccoli and Baby Corn*

# BRAISED MUSHROOMS WITH LETTUCE

## 4 SERVINGS

3/4 ounce dried black (shiitake) mushrooms (about 15)

1 medium head iceberg lettuce (about 1 pound)

1 tablespoon cornstarch

1 tablespoon water

1 teaspoon sugar

1/2 teaspoon salt

1 teaspoon sesame oil

1 1/2 cups fat-free reduced-sodium chicken broth

2 tablespoons soy sauce

Soak mushrooms in hot water about 20 minutes or until soft; drain. Rinse with warm water; drain. Squeeze out excess moisture. Remove and discard stems; cut caps into 1/2-inch strips. Tear head of lettuce into fourths; separate into leaves. Mix cornstarch, water, sugar and salt.

Spray nonstick wok or 3-quart saucepan with nonstick cooking spray; heat over medium-high heat until cooking spray starts to bubble. Add sesame oil; rotate wok to coat side. Add mushrooms; stir-fry 30 seconds. Add broth and soy sauce; heat to boiling. Add lettuce; cook uncovered 2 minutes, stirring constantly.

Add cornstarch mixture to wok; cook and stir until sauce is thickened.

*1 package (16 ounces) salad mix can be substituted for the iceberg lettuce.

| 1 Serving: | | % Daily Value: | |
|---|---|---|---|
| Calories | 60 | Vitamin A | 4% |
| Calories from fat | 20 | Vitamin C | 6% |
| Fat, g | 2 | Calcium | 2% |
| Saturated, g | 0 | Iron | 10% |
| Cholesterol, mg | 0 | **Diet Exchanges:** | |
| Sodium, mg | 960 | Vegetable | 2 |
| Carbohydrate, g | 10 | | |
| Dietary Fiber, g | 2 | | |
| Protein, g | 3 | | |

# RED-COOKED SQUASH

## 6 SERVINGS

*Kabocha is an Oriental squash with a sweet, buttery flavor and daikon is a long, white Oriental radish that has a crisp, fresh crunch. Both are becoming more readily available and add authenticity to this recipe when available. Red-cooking is a traditional low-fat Chinese cooking technique that uses soy sauce to give foods intense color and flavor.*

1 1/2 ounces dried black (shiitake) mushrooms

2 Green Onion Flowers (page 9)

1 medium kabocha or buttercup squash (2 1/2 pounds)

1 cup fat-free reduced-sodium chicken broth

1/4 cup mushroom soy sauce

1 tablespoon hoisin sauce

1 teaspoon sugar

2 cloves garlic, finely chopped

1 cup grated daikon radish, if desired

Soak mushrooms in hot water about 20 minutes or until soft; drain. Meanwhile, prepare Green Onion Flowers. Cut squash into fourths; peel.* Cut squash into 2-inch strips; cut strips into 1/4-inch slices. Rinse mushrooms with warm water; drain. Squeeze out excess moisture. Remove and discard stems; cut caps into slices.

Place mushrooms and squash in 12-inch nonstick skillet. Mix broth, soy sauce, hoisin sauce, sugar and garlic; pour over squash. Heat to boiling; reduce heat to medium-low. Cover and cook about 10 minutes or until squash is tender. Garnish with daikon and Green Onion Flowers.

*To soften squash shell for cutting, pierce shell several times with a knife. Microwave on High 3 minutes.

| 1 Serving: | | % Daily Value: | |
|---|---|---|---|
| Calories | 75 | Vitamin A | 52% |
| Calories from fat | 10 | Vitamin C | 14% |
| Fat, g | 1 | Calcium | 2% |
| Saturated, g | 0 | Iron | 8% |
| Cholesterol, mg | 0 | **Diet Exchanges:** | |
| Sodium, mg | 760 | Vegetable | 1 |
| Carbohydrate, g | 18 | Fruit | 1 |
| Dietary Fiber, g | 5 | | |
| Protein, g | 3 | | |

# VEGETABLE KUNG PAO

### 4 SERVINGS

**1/2 cup partially defatted roasted peanuts or 1/4 cup dry-roasted peanuts**

**1 tablespoon cornstarch**

**1 teaspoon sugar**

**1 tablespoon cold water**

**1/2 cup fat-free reduced-sodium chicken broth**

**1 teaspoon chile puree with garlic**

**1 package (16 ounces) frozen broccoli, carrots, red peppers with garbanzo and other beans**

Spray nonstick wok or 12-inch skillet with non-stick cooking spray; heat over medium-high heat until cooking spray starts to bubble. Spread peanuts in single layer on paper towel; spray lightly with cooking spray, about 2 seconds. Add to wok; stir-fry about 1 minute or until toasted. Immediately remove from wok; cool.

Mix cornstarch, sugar and cold water; set aside. Mix broth and chile puree in wok; heat to boiling. Stir in vegetables. Heat to boiling; reduce heat to medium-low. Cover and cook 5 minutes, stirring several times.

Move vegetables to side of wok. Stir cornstarch mixture into liquid in skillet. Cook and stir vegetables and sauce over high heat about 1 minute or until sauce is thickened. Stir in peanuts.

| 1 Serving: | | % Daily Value: | |
|---|---|---|---|
| Calories | 150 | Vitamin A | 80% |
| Calories from fat | 35 | Vitamin C | 24% |
| Fat, g | 4 | Calcium | 4% |
| Saturated, g | 0 | Iron | 8% |
| Cholesterol, mg | 0 | **Diet Exchanges:** | |
| Sodium, mg | 300 | Starch/bread | 1 |
| Carbohydrate, g | 19 | Lean meat | 1 |
| Dietary Fiber, g | 0 | Vegetable | 1 |
| Protein, g | 10 | | |

# SPICY SWEET POTATO WITH FRAGRANT GREEN

**4** SERVINGS

*The Chinese call cilantro "Fragrant Green." Highly flavored seasonings like cilantro and chile sauce allow us to reduce the fat in a recipe while pumping up the flavor and achieving true taste satisfaction.*

**1/2 cup fat-free reduced-sodium chicken broth**

**2 tablespoons red wine vinegar**

**1 tablespoon dark soy sauce**

**1 teaspoon sugar**

**Dash of pepper**

**1 1/2 pounds sweet potatoes (3 large), peeled and cut into 1/2-inch cubes (5 cups)**

**2 teaspoons vegetable oil**

**2 teaspoons chile puree with garlic**

**2 teaspoons grated gingerroot**

**2 tablespoons chopped fresh cilantro**

Mix broth, vinegar, soy sauce, sugar and pepper. Spray nonstick wok or 12-inch skillet with nonstick cooking spray; heat over medium-high heat until cooking spray starts to bubble. Add sweet potatoes; stir-fry 2 minutes. Move potatoes to side of wok. Add oil to wok; stir in chile puree and gingerroot. Stir-fry potatoes 1 minute.

Stir in broth mixture. Heat to boiling; reduce heat to medium-low. Cover and cook about 10 minutes or until potatoes are tender. Stir in cilantro.

| 1 Serving: | | % Daily Value: | |
|---|---|---|---|
| Calories | 130 | Vitamin A | 100% |
| Calories from fat | 20 | Vitamin C | 20% |
| Fat, g | 2 | Calcium | 2% |
| Saturated, g | 0 | Iron | 4% |
| Cholesterol, mg | 0 | **Diet Exchanges:** | |
| Sodium, mg | 350 | Starch/bread | 1 |
| Carbohydrate, g | 28 | Vegetable | 2 |
| Dietary Fiber, g | 2 | | |
| Protein, g | 2 | | |

*Spicy Sweet Potato with Fragrant Green,*
*Five-Spice Turkey Breast (page 51)*

# BOK CHOY WITH BAKED TOFU

### 4 SERVINGS

**1 package (14 ounces) firm lite tofu**

**8 large stalks bok choy**

**2 tablespoons soy sauce**

**1 teaspoon sugar**

**1/2 teaspoon garlic powder**

**1 teaspoon vegetable oil**

**3 shallots, thinly sliced**

**1/4 teaspoon salt**

**2 tablespoons oyster sauce**

Wrap tofu in kitchen towel; cover with plastic wrap. Place heavy weight on top; let stand 30 minutes to press out excess moisture. Cut tofu into 1 × 1 × 1/4-inch pieces.

Remove leaves from bok choy stems. Cut leaves into 2-inch pieces; cut stems into 1/4-inch diagonal slices. Mix soy sauce, sugar and garlic powder.

Heat oven to 425°. Line cookie sheet with aluminum foil. Place tofu on foil, brushing with soy sauce mixture. Bake 5 minutes. Spray tofu with cooking spray; bake about 2 minutes or until brown. Turn tofu over; bake 5 minutes longer.

Meanwhile, spray nonstick wok or 12-inch skillet with nonstick cooking spray; heat over medium-high heat until cooking spray starts to bubble. Add oil; rotate wok to coat side. Add bok choy and shallots; stir-fry 1 minute. Add salt, tofu and oyster sauce; cover and cook 1 minute.

| 1 Serving: | | % Daily Value: | |
| --- | --- | --- | --- |
| Calories | 100 | Vitamin A | 44% |
| Calories from fat | 35 | Vitamin C | 52% |
| Fat, g | 4 | Calcium | 36% |
| Saturated, g | 0 | Iron | 68% |
| Cholesterol, mg | 0 | **Diet Exchanges:** | |
| Sodium, mg | 1140 | Lean meat | 1 |
| Carbohydrate, g | 8 | Vegetable | 2 |
| Dietary Fiber, g | 4 | | |
| Protein, g | 12 | | |

*Bok Choy with Baked Tofu*

# SHREDDED HUNAN VEGETABLES

### 4 SERVINGS

**2 tablespoons rice vinegar**

**1 tablespoon soy sauce**

**1 teaspoon chile puree or Easy Sichuan Sauce (page 124)**

**1 teaspoon grated gingerroot**

**1 teaspoon cornstarch**

**1 teaspoon cold water**

**2 teaspoons chile oil**

**3 medium carrots, shredded (2 cups)**

**2 cups shredded zucchini (2 medium)**

**2 medium stalks celery, cut into 1/4-inch diagonal slices (1 cup)**

**1 package (8 ounces) fresh bean sprouts or 1 can (14 to 16 ounces) bean sprouts, rinsed and drained**

**8 whole unblanched almonds**

Mix vinegar, soy sauce, chile puree and gingerroot in medium bowl. Mix cornstarch and cold water; stir into vinegar mixture.

Spray nonstick wok or 12-inch skillet with nonstick cooking spray; heat over medium-high heat until cooking spray starts to bubble. Add chile oil; rotate wok to coat side. Add carrots and zucchini; stir-fry 1 minute. Add celery and bean sprouts; stir-fry 1 minute. Stir vinegar mixture; stir into carrot mixture. Cook and stir about 1 minute or until sauce is thickened. Top with almonds.

| 1 Serving: | | % Daily Value: | |
| --- | --- | --- | --- |
| Calories | 160 | Vitamin A | 88% |
| Calories from fat | 70 | Vitamin C | 20% |
| Fat, g | 8 | Calcium | 8% |
| Saturated, g | 1 | Iron | 12% |
| Cholesterol, mg | 0 | **Diet Exchanges:** | |
| Sodium, mg | 320 | Vegetable | 3 |
| Carbohydrate, g | 18 | Fat | 2 |
| Dietary Fiber, g | 6 | | |
| Protein, g | 10 | | |

# 6

# SAUCES AND CONDIMENTS

*Mongolian Firepot (page 87), Hot Mustard Sauce (page 123), Lime Dipping Sauce (page 120), Sweet-and-Sour Plum Sauce (page 122)*

# ♥ CILANTRO DIPPING SAUCE

ABOUT **1** CUP SAUCE

1/3 cup lemon juice

2 tablespoons vegetable oil

1/4 cup packed fresh cilantro leaves

1/4 cup packed fresh parsley sprigs

1 1/2 teaspoons paprika

1 teaspoon ground cumin

1/8 to 1/4 teaspoon ground red pepper (cayenne)

Salt and pepper to taste

Place all ingredients in blender or food processor. Cover; blend on medium to high speed until smooth.

| 1 Tablespoon: | | % Daily Value: | |
| --- | --- | --- | --- |
| Calories | 20 | Vitamin A | 2% |
| Calories from fat | 20 | Vitamin C | 4% |
| Fat, g | 2 | Calcium | 0% |
| Saturated, g | 0 | Iron | 0% |
| Cholesterol, mg | 0 | **Diet Exchanges:** | |
| Sodium, mg | 35 | Free food | |
| Carbohydrate, g | 1 | | |
| Dietary Fiber, g | 0 | | |
| Protein, g | 0 | | |

# ♥ HOISIN DIPPING SAUCE

ABOUT **1/4** CUP SAUCE

1/4 cup hoisin sauce

1 1/2 teaspoons lime juice or rice vinegar

Mix ingredients.

| 1 Tablespoon: | | % Daily Value: | |
| --- | --- | --- | --- |
| Calories | 35 | Vitamin A | 2% |
| Calories from fat | 10 | Vitamin C | 12% |
| Fat, g | 1 | Calcium | 0% |
| Saturated, g | 0 | Iron | 2% |
| Cholesterol, mg | 0 | **Diet Exchanges:** | |
| Sodium, mg | 2 | Vegetable | 1 |
| Carbohydrate, g | 5 | | |
| Dietary Fiber, g | 0 | | |
| Protein, g | 1 | | |

# ♥ LEMON DIPPING SAUCE

ABOUT **1/3** CUP SAUCE

*This dipping sauce takes on totally different flavors by simply varying the citrus fruit used, such as grapefruit or tangerine.*

3 tablespoons soy sauce

2 tablespoons seasoned rice vinegar

2 teaspoons garlic, finely chopped

1/2 teaspoon grated lemon peel

Shake all ingredients in tightly covered container until well mixed.

**LIME DIPPING SAUCE:** Substitute grated lime peel for lemon peel.

**ORANGE DIPPING SAUCE:** Substitute grated orange peel for lemon peel. Add 1 teaspoon chopped fresh cilantro leaves if desired.

| 1 Tablespoon | | % Daily Value: | |
| --- | --- | --- | --- |
| Calories | 10 | Vitamin A | 0% |
| Calories from fat | 0 | Vitamin C | 0% |
| Fat, g | 0 | Calcium | 0% |
| Saturated, g | 0 | Iron | 0% |
| Cholesterol, mg | 0 | **Diet Exchanges:** | |
| Sodium, mg | 510 | Free food | |
| Carbohydrate, g | 1 | | |
| Dietary Fiber, g | 0 | | |
| Protein, g | 1 | | |

# ♥ HORSERADISH DIPPING SAUCE

ABOUT 1/2 CUP SAUCE

*This adds a bit of zing to any mild-flavored dumpling, such as Steamed Vegetable Dumplings (page 15).*

**1/4 cup soy sauce**

**2 tablespoons prepared horseradish**

**2 teaspoons grated gingerroot**

**1 teaspoon sugar**

**1 1/2 teaspoons rice vinegar**

Mix all ingredients.

| 1 Tablespoon: | | % Daily Value: | |
|---|---|---|---|
| Calories | 10 | Vitamin A | 0% |
| Calories from fat | 0 | Vitamin C | 0% |
| Fat, g | 0 | Calcium | 0% |
| Saturated, g | 0 | Iron | 0% |
| Cholesterol, mg | 0 | **Diet Exchanges:** | |
| Sodium, mg | 520 | Free food | |
| Carbohydrate, g | 2 | | |
| Dietary Fiber, g | 0 | | |
| Protein, g | 1 | | |

# ♥ CHINESE LEMON SAUCE

ABOUT 3/4 CUP SAUCE

*This is the sauce that gives Baked Lemon Chicken (page 34) its sweet-tangy flavor. It is also great served cold as a dipping sauce for egg rolls and wontons.*

**1/3 cup fat-free reduced-sodium chicken broth**

**1/4 cup sugar**

**1 1/2 teaspoons grated lemon peel**

**3 tablespoons lemon juice**

**2 tablespoons light corn syrup**

**2 tablespoons rice vinegar**

**1 clove garlic, finely chopped or 1/2 teaspoon garlic powder**

**1/4 teaspoon salt**

**2 teaspoons cornstarch**

**2 teaspoons cold water**

Heat broth, sugar, lemon peel, lemon juice, corn syrup, vinegar, garlic and salt to boiling in 1-quart saucepan, stirring occasionally. Mix cornstarch and cold water; stir into sauce. Cook and stir about 30 seconds or until thickened. Serve warm, or cover and refrigerate up to 2 weeks.

| 3 Tablespoons: | | % Daily Value: | |
|---|---|---|---|
| Calories | 90 | Vitamin A | 0% |
| Calories from fat | 0 | Vitamin C | 2% |
| Fat, g | 0 | Calcium | 0% |
| Saturated, g | 0 | Iron | 0% |
| Cholesterol, mg | 0 | **Diet Exchanges:** | |
| Sodium, mg | 180 | Fruit | 1 1/2 |
| Carbohydrate, g | 23 | | |
| Dietary Fiber, g | 0 | | |
| Protein, g | 0 | | |

## ♥ ORANGE-GINGER SAUCE

ABOUT **1/2** CUP SAUCE

*Use this citrus sauce as you would any sweet-and-sour dipping sauce. The dried bell pepper flakes can be found in the spice section of the supermarket.*

**1/4 cup seasoned rice vinegar**

**2 tablespoons peanut or vegetable oil**

**1 teaspoon grated orange peel**

**2 tablespoons orange juice**

**1 tablespoon honey**

**2 cloves garlic, finely chopped**

**1 teaspoon dried bell pepper flakes, if desired**

**1/2 teaspoon grated gingerroot**

Shake all ingredients in tightly covered container until well mixed.

| 1 Serving: | | % Daily Value: | |
|---|---|---|---|
| Calories | 40 | Vitamin A | 0% |
| Calories from fat | 25 | Vitamin C | 2% |
| Fat, g | 3 | Calcium | 0% |
| Saturated, g | 1 | Iron | 0% |
| Cholesterol, mg | 0 | **Diet Exchanges:** | |
| Sodium, mg | 0 | Fat | 1 |
| Carbohydrate, g | 3 | | |
| Dietary Fiber, g | 0 | | |
| Protein, g | 0 | | |

## ♥ SWEET-AND-SOUR PLUM SAUCE

ABOUT **1 1/4** CUPS SAUCE

*(photograph on page 13)*

*Use this sauce for dipping egg rolls, served over grilled or steamed meat or in any recipe calling for a sweet-and-sour or duck sauce. Duck (or duk) sauce is the Chinese name for plum sauce, and though it is delicious on duck or other poultry, it does not contain any poultry products.*

**1 cup plum preserves or jelly**

**2 tablespoons ketchup**

**2 tablespoons unseasoned or seasoned rice vinegar**

Heat all ingredients in 1-quart saucepan over medium heat about 2 minutes, stirring frequently, until heated through. Serve hot, or cover and refrigerate at least 1 hour.

**SWEET-HOT PLUM SAUCE:** Substitute chile puree for the ketchup.

| 1 Tablespoon: | | % Daily Value: | |
|---|---|---|---|
| Calories | 45 | Vitamin A | 0% |
| Calories from fat | 0 | Vitamin C | 0% |
| Fat, g | 0 | Calcium | 0% |
| Saturated, g | 0 | Iron | 0% |
| Cholesterol, mg | 0 | **Diet Exchanges:** | |
| Sodium, mg | 25 | Fruit | 1 |
| Carbohydrate, g | 11 | | |
| Dietary Fiber, g | 0 | | |
| Protein, g | 0 | | |

 ## HOT MUSTARD SAUCE

ABOUT 1/4 CUP SAUCE

*(photograph on page 13)*

**3 tablespoons ground mustard (dry)**
**2 tablespoons water**
**1 tablespoon seasoned rice vinegar**

Mix all ingredients. Cover and let stand 5 minutes. Make sauce for same-day use; strength increases and quality decreases when stored.

| 1 Teaspoon: | | % Daily Value: | |
|---|---|---|---|
| Calories | 0 | Vitamin A | 0% |
| Calories from fat | 0 | Vitamin C | 0% |
| Fat, g | 0 | Calcium | 0% |
| Saturated, g | 0 | Iron | 0% |
| Cholesterol, mg | 0 | **Diet Exchanges:** | |
| Sodium, mg | 0 | Free food | |
| Carbohydrate, g | 0 | | |
| Dietary Fiber, g | 0 | | |
| Protein, g | 0 | | |

 ## HOT-SWEET APRICOT MUSTARD

ABOUT 3/4 CUP MUSTARD

**1/2 cup apricot spreadable fruit**
**2 tablespoons Chinese hot mustard**
**1 tablespoon lemon or lime juice**
**1 teaspoon grated gingerroot**

Mix all ingredients.

| 1 Tablespoon: | | % Daily Value: | |
|---|---|---|---|
| Calories | 30 | Vitamin A | 0% |
| Calories from fat | 0 | Vitamin C | 2% |
| Fat, g | 0 | Calcium | 0% |
| Saturated, g | 0 | Iron | 0% |
| Cholesterol, mg | 0 | **Diet Exchanges:** | |
| Sodium, mg | 30 | Fruit | 1/2 |
| Carbohydrate, g | 8 | | |
| Dietary Fiber, g | 1 | | |
| Protein, g | 0 | | |

 ## LIME-MUSTARD SAUCE

ABOUT 1/3 CUP SAUCE

**1/4 cup Chinese hot mustard**
**1/2 teaspoon grated lime peel**
**1 tablespoon lime juice**

Mix all ingredients.

| 1 Teaspoon: | | % Daily Value: | |
|---|---|---|---|
| Calories | 0 | Vitamin A | 0% |
| Calories from fat | 0 | Vitamin C | 0% |
| Fat, g | 0 | Calcium | 0% |
| Saturated, g | 0 | Iron | 0% |
| Cholesterol, mg | 0 | **Diet Exchanges:** | |
| Sodium, mg | 45 | Free food | |
| Carbohydrate, g | 0 | | |
| Dietary Fiber, g | 0 | | |
| Protein, g | 0 | | |

 ## HONEY SICHUAN SAUCE

ABOUT 2/3 CUP SAUCE

**1/3 cup honey**
**1/3 cup chile puree**

Mix ingredients.

| 1 Tablespoon: | | % Daily Value: | |
|---|---|---|---|
| Calories | 45 | Vitamin A | 0% |
| Calories from fat | 0 | Vitamin C | 2% |
| Fat, g | 0 | Calcium | 0% |
| Saturated, g | 0 | Iron | 0% |
| Cholesterol, mg | 0 | **Diet Exchanges:** | |
| Sodium, mg | 95 | Fruit | 1 |
| Carbohydrate, g | 11 | | |
| Dietary Fiber, g | 0 | | |
| Protein, g | 0 | | |

 ## GARLIC STIR-FRY SAUCE

ABOUT 1/2 CUP SAUCE

*This basic, easy sauce will turn most any meat and vegetable combination into a delicious stir-fry.*

**1/3 cup fat-free reduced-sodium chicken broth**

**1 tablespoon soy sauce**

**4 cloves garlic, finely chopped**

**2 teaspoons grated gingerroot**

**2 teaspoons cornstarch**

**1 teaspoon sugar**

**2 teaspoons water**

Mix broth, soy sauce, garlic and gingerroot in small bowl. Mix cornstarch, sugar and water; stir into broth mixture. Pour into wok over enough stir-fried meat and vegetables for 4 servings. Stir-fry over medium-high heat about 1 minute or until thickened.

**SPICY GARLIC STIR-FRY SAUCE:** Add 1 to 2 teaspoons chile puree to broth mixture.

| 1 Tablespoon: | | % Daily Value: | |
|---|---|---|---|
| Calories | 10 | Vitamin A | 0% |
| Calories from fat | 0 | Vitamin C | 0% |
| Fat, g | 0 | Calcium | 0% |
| Saturated, g | 0 | Iron | 0% |
| Cholesterol, mg | 0 | **Diet Exchanges:** | |
| Sodium, mg | 290 | Free food | |
| Carbohydrate, g | 3 | | |
| Dietary Fiber, g | 0 | | |
| Protein, g | 0 | | |

 ## EASY SICHUAN SAUCE

ABOUT 1/2 CUP SAUCE

*Use this sauce to season a stir-fry, such as Chicken Sichuan with Spinach (page 42), where you want a little kick.*

**1/4 cup fat-free reduced-sodium chicken broth**

**1 tablespoon hoisin sauce**

**1 tablespoon soy sauce**

**1 tablespoon chile puree**

**2 teaspoons seasoned or unseasoned rice vinegar**

**1 teaspoon grated gingerroot**

**1/8 teaspoon ground red pepper (cayenne)**

Shake all ingredients in tightly covered container until well mixed.

| 1 Tablespoon | | % Daily Value: | |
|---|---|---|---|
| Calories | 5 | Vitamin A | 0% |
| Calories from fat | 0 | Vitamin C | 0% |
| Fat, g | 0 | Calcium | 0% |
| Saturated, g | 0 | Iron | 0% |
| Cholesterol, mg | 0 | **Diet Exchanges:** | |
| Sodium, mg | 160 | Free food | |
| Carbohydrate, g | 1 | | |
| Dietary Fiber, g | 0 | | |
| Protein, g | 0 | | |

# ♥ BLACK BEAN SAUCE

ABOUT **1** CUP SAUCE

*This all-purpose black bean sauce can be spooned over stir-fried or steamed fish, shellfish or poultry.*

**2 tablespoons fermented black beans, rinsed**

**1 tablespoon grated gingerroot**

**2 cloves garlic, finely chopped**

**3/4 cup fat-free reduced-sodium chicken broth**

**2 teaspoons cornstarch**

**1 teaspoon sugar**

**Dash of pepper**

**2 tablespoons dry sherry or fat-free reduced-sodium chicken broth**

**2 tablespoons dark soy sauce**

**1/2 teaspoon sesame oil**

Mash beans, gingerroot and garlic together with back of spoon in small bowl. Mix broth, cornstarch, sugar, pepper, sherry, soy sauce and sesame oil.

Spray 1-quart nonstick saucepan with nonstick cooking spray; heat over medium-high heat until cooking spray starts to bubble. Add bean mixture; cook and stir 30 seconds. Add broth mixture; cook about 2 minutes, stirring constantly, until thickened.

| **1/4 Cup:** | | **% Daily Value:** | |
|---|---|---|---|
| Calories | 50 | Vitamin A | 0% |
| Calories from fat | 10 | Vitamin C | 0% |
| Fat, g | 1 | Calcium | 2% |
| Saturated, g | 0 | Iron | 4% |
| Cholesterol, mg | 0 | **Diet Exchanges:** | |
| Sodium, mg | 600 | Vegetable | 2 |
| Carbohydrate, g | 9 | | |
| Dietary Fiber, g | 1 | | |
| Protein, g | 2 | | |

# ♥ BROWN BEAN–PEANUT SAUCE

ABOUT **1 1/2** CUPS SAUCE

*This spunky sauce adds a bit of fire to mild dishes.*

**1/4 cup brown bean paste**

**1 cup water**

**1 tablespoon tomato paste**

**1 tablespoon creamy peanut butter**

**1 tablespoon soy sauce**

**1 1/2 teaspoons sugar**

**1 teaspoon chile puree with garlic**

**2 cloves garlic, finely chopped**

Mix all ingredients in 1-quart saucepan with wire whisk. Heat to boiling; reduce heat. Simmer 2 minutes, stirring constantly.

| **2 Tablespoons:** | | **% Daily Value:** | |
|---|---|---|---|
| Calories | 20 | Vitamin A | 0% |
| Calories from fat | 10 | Vitamin C | 0% |
| Fat, g | 1 | Calcium | 0% |
| Saturated, g | 0 | Iron | 0% |
| Cholesterol, mg | 0 | **Diet Exchanges:** | |
| Sodium, mg | 150 | Free food | |
| Carbohydrate, g | 2 | | |
| Dietary Fiber, g | 0 | | |
| Protein, g | 1 | | |

# ♥ SPICY PEANUT BUTTER SAUCE

ABOUT 3/4 CUP SAUCE

*Add a spark to noodles or pour over rice.*

**2 teaspoons ground mustard (dry)**

**2 teaspoons water**

**2 tablespoons reduced-fat peanut butter**

**3 tablespoons water**

**2 tablespoons dark soy sauce**

**1/4 cup lime juice**

**2 tablespoons sugar**

**1 dried small hot chile, crushed, or 1/2 teaspoon dried crushed red pepper**

Mix mustard and 2 teaspoons water with wire whisk or fork in small bowl. Stir in peanut butter. Stir in 3 tablespoons water and the soy sauce until blended. Stir in lime juice and sugar, a small amount at a time, until blended. Stir in crushed chile.

| 2 Tablespoons: | | % Daily Value: | |
|---|---|---|---|
| Calories | 55 | Vitamin A | 6% |
| Calories from fat | 20 | Vitamin C | 14% |
| Fat, g | 2 | Calcium | 0% |
| Saturated, g | 1 | Iron | 2% |
| Cholesterol, mg | 0 | **Diet Exchanges:** | |
| Sodium, mg | 370 | Starch/bread | 1/2 |
| Carbohydrate, g | 7 | | |
| Dietary Fiber, g | 0 | | |
| Protein, g | 2 | | |

# ♥ WARM PEANUT DRESSING

ABOUT 3/4 CUP DRESSING

*You can easily turn this delicious peanut dressing into a more mellow sauce than Spicy Peanut Butter Sauce by increasing the cornstarch to one tablespoon; toss with noodles or pour over rice. We added bell pepper to it when we made it a sauce in Noodle Pancakes with Peanut Sauce (page 106).*

**1/3 cup unsweetened pineapple juice**

**1/4 cup water**

**1 1/4 teaspoons ground coriander**

**1 teaspoon cornstarch**

**2 cloves garlic, finely chopped**

**2 tablespoons creamy peanut butter**

**1 1/2 tablespoons cider vinegar**

**2 teaspoons soy sauce**

**1 1/2 teaspoons grated gingerroot**

Heat all ingredients to boiling in 1-quart saucepan, stirring constantly. Stir until smooth; remove from heat. Let stand 5 minutes.

| 2 Tablespoons: | | % Daily Value: | |
|---|---|---|---|
| Calories | 45 | Vitamin A | 0% |
| Calories from fat | 25 | Vitamin C | 0% |
| Fat, g | 3 | Calcium | 0% |
| Saturated, g | 1 | Iron | 2% |
| Cholesterol, mg | 0 | **Diet Exchanges:** | |
| Sodium, mg | 140 | Vegetable | 1 |
| Carbohydrate, g | 4 | | |
| Dietary Fiber, g | 0 | | |
| Protein, g | 1 | | |

#  PICKLED GINGERROOT

*Quickly flavor foods with either the ginger slices or its pickling liquid. Pickled ginger can be cut into fine strips and served with grilled meats and vegetables or tossed into a stir-fry. Look for smooth, tight and thin-skinned young ginger for pickling.*

**1/4 cup sugar**

**1 cup fat-free reduced-sodium chicken broth**

**1/2 cup seasoned or unseasoned rice vinegar**

**2 tablespoons dry sherry or rice wine, if desired**

**1/4 pound gingerroot, peeled and very thinly sliced**

Heat sugar, broth, vinegar and sherry to boiling in 1-quart saucepan, stirring frequently until sugar is dissolved. Stir in gingerroot; remove from heat. Cool 15 minutes. Cover and refrigerate at least 24 hours or up to 3 months.

| 2 Slices and 1/2 Tablespoon Liquid: | | % Daily Value: | |
|---|---|---|---|
| Calories | 10 | Vitamin A | 0% |
| Calories from fat | 0 | Vitamin C | 0% |
| Fat, g | 0 | Calcium | 0% |
| Saturated, g | 0 | Iron | 0% |
| Cholesterol, mg | 0 | **Diet Exchanges:** | |
| Sodium, mg | 10 | Free food | |
| Carbohydrate, g | 2 | | |
| Dietary Fiber, g | 0 | | |
| Protein, g | 0 | | |

#  CUCUMBER RELISH

*Pair this cool, crisp relish with any Chinese dish.*

**2 medium cucumbers, peeled, seeded and very thinly sliced**

**2 tablespoons finely chopped pickled ginger**

**2 tablespoons pickled ginger juice**

**2 tablespoons seasoned rice vinegar**

**2 teaspoons white or black sesame seed, lightly toasted**

Mix all ingredients. Cover and refrigerate at least 1 hour.

| 1/4 cup: | | % Daily Value: | |
|---|---|---|---|
| Calories | 10 | Vitamin A | 0% |
| Calories from fat | 0 | Vitamin C | 4% |
| Fat, g | 0 | Calcium | 0% |
| Saturated, g | 0 | Iron | 0% |
| Cholesterol, mg | 0 | **Diet Exchanges:** | |
| Sodium, mg | 2 | Free food | |
| Carbohydrate, g | 2 | | |
| Dietary Fiber, g | 0 | | |
| Protein, g | 0 | | |

# GLOSSARY OF COMMON INGREDIENTS

**Bamboo Shoots.** The young, tender, ivory-colored shoots from the tropical bamboo plant are eaten as a vegetable. Fresh bamboo can be purchased, but most of us are familiar with the canned. They can be purchased whole, sliced or in chunks, or in water-packed form. The tender, pointed end of the shoot is used for stir-frying. The wide, less tender end is used for soups and stews or can be sliced very thin for stir-frying. To store bamboo shoots, cover with cold water in a tightly covered jar and refrigerate. Change the water daily.

**Barbecue Sauce, Chinese** (barbecue and roasting sauce). This is Hoisin Sauce with sweetened tomato sauce or a fruit flavor. Hoisin Sauce can be substituted.

**Bean Sprouts.** Young, white sprouts of the mung bean have a crisp texture and delicate flavor and can be found fresh or canned. Just prior to cooking, they should be rinsed in cold water to retain their crispness. Store fresh sprouts covered with cold water in a covered container in the refrigerator; use them within four days.

**Black Beans, Fermented** (salted black beans). Small, black fermented soybeans have a strong, pungent, salty flavor. Major grocery stores have fermented black beans in small cardboard boxes but look for jars, cans or plastic bags of various sizes at Asian markets. To remove excess salt, stir the beans in warm water for 2 minutes, then drain well. Refrigerate, tightly covered, after opening. Brown bean sauce can be substituted.

**Bok Choy** (Chinese chard or white mustard cabbage). This vegetable resembles both chard and cabbage, with crisp, white stalks and shiny, green leaves. It is used primarily in soups and stir-fried dishes. The leaves are easily separated from the stalks and should be added last to dishes to avoid overcooking. Bok choy is sold by the pound.

**Brown Bean Sauce** (bean sauce, brown bean paste or ground bean sauce). A thick, salty sauce made from fermented yellow soybeans, flour and salt, brown bean sauce adds flavor to cooked meats or sauces. The sauce is generally available in two forms: one version contains the whole bean and the second is smaller and is made from ground beans. Both are sold in jars. Whole beans should be mashed before using. Refrigerate, tightly covered, after opening. Dark soy sauce can be substituted. **Hot Bean Sauce** (spicy brown bean sauce) is flavored with hot chili peppers.

**Chile Oil** (hot chile oil, hot oil or hot stir-fry oil). This is a fiery hot vegetable or sesame oil infused with the flavors of hot chile peppers. To make your own hot oil, heat an 8-inch skillet until hot. Add 3 tablespoons vegetable oil and 1 teaspoon cayenne pepper. Heat over medium heat 5 minutes. Remove from heat; let stand until cool. Pour through a strainer lined with a paper coffee filter or paper towel. Store, tightly covered, in the refrigerator. Store-bought chile oil can be refrigerated too. Both will keep longer in the refrigerator. You'll find commercial chile oil in the Oriental foods section of major grocery stores, Asian markets and gourmet shops.

**Chile Puree** (Chinese chile sauce, chile sauce or Chinese chile paste). This hot, spicy sauce is made from chilies, soybeans, salt, oil and garlic. It is used to put the fire in many Sichuan or Hunan dishes and is used both as a seasoning and a condiment. To make chile paste, heat an 8-inch skillet over medium-high heat until hot. Add 1 tablespoon vegetable oil. Stir in 1/4 cup ground

1. Chinese Cabbage   2. Bean Sprouts   3. Dried Black Mushrooms   4. Water Chestnuts   5. Jalapeño Peppers   6. Rice Vinegar
7. Sesame Oil   8. Lo Mein Noodles   9. Bok Choy   10. Straw Mushrooms   11. Jicama   12. Rice Stix Noodles   13. Thai
Peppers   14. Daikon Radish   15. Dry Mustard   16. Gingerroot   17. Chinese Noodles   18. Converted White Rice   19. Garlic
20. Cayenne Peppers   21. Cilantro

brown bean sauce, 1 teaspoon ground red pepper, 1 tablespoon sugar and 1 tablespoon finely chopped gingerroot. Reduce heat to low. Cook 10 minutes, stirring frequently so it does not burn. **Chile Puree with Garlic** contains garlic. **Sweet Chile Sauce** (sweet-hot chile sauce) is a sweet version of chile puree. It may be sweetened with sugar or citrus fruit. If unavailable, add sugar or pineapple juice to chile puree.

**Chilies, Dried** (dried chile peppers). Spicy red chilies, either crushed or whole, are sold in spice bottles in most grocery stores. They add a hot flavor common to Hunan and Sichuan foods. Since they can be kept indefinitely without refrigeration, they are often used in place of fresh chilies. If using dried chilies instead of fresh, use only 1/4 the amount of fresh chilies that the recipe calls for. See also **Chilies, Fresh**.

**Chilies, Fresh** (chile peppers). When selecting fresh chilies, look for those that are glossy, plump and unblemished. Chilies commonly found in the produce section of grocery stores and used in Chinese cooking are: red fresno or green jalapeños, serranos and tiny green or red Thai peppers. Chilies vary greatly in heat, with the smallest varieties being the hottest. Wear thin plastic gloves or oil your hands to prevent volatile oils from burning your hands and sensitive areas such as your eyes, which you may later touch. If the seeds and ribs of chilies are used it will greatly increase the heat of the chilies. Fresh chilies can be refrigerated for at least two weeks. See also **Chilies, Dried**.

**Chinese Cabbage** (Napa cabbage, celery cabbage or sui choy). The dense, oblong heads of celery cabbage feature long, smooth stalks with pale green leaves.

**Cilantro** (Chinese parsley or fresh coriander). The leaf of this strongly and distinctly flavored aromatic herb has a tangy citrus flavor with a slight soapy taste that gives a zing of freshness when added to sauces or sprinkled over food just before serving. It has no flavor dried, so it should always be used fresh. It is available in the produce department of major grocery stores, Asian markets and farmers' markets. To store, place a bunch in a jar of water, stems down; make a fresh cut on the stems every other day. Cover leaves with a plastic bag wrapped tightly around the top of the jar. Refrigerate up to 2 weeks. Chop or cut leaves with scissors. There is no substitute.

**Coconut Milk, Reduced-Fat.** Coconut milk is valued for its rich, exotic flavor. Canned coconut milk is sold in major grocery stores in the Oriental foods aisle (often it is sold with canned milk) or in Asian markets. The reduced-fat versions are usually labeled "lite" and have 1/3 to 1/2 the fat grams of regular coconut milk. Coconut is one of the few plant sources of saturated fat—so it is used sparingly in a low-fat diet. Do not use sweet cream of coconut, which is used for drinks like piña coladas. To make your own low-fat coconut milk, heat 1 cup 1% milk with 1/4 cup shredded,

unsweetened coconut meat (not sweetened coconut flakes) to boiling. Let stand 15 minutes; strain coconut and discard. Unsweetened coconut meat can be purchased dried or frozen at food cooperatives or Asian markets, or can be shredded from a fresh coconut.

**Coriander, Ground.** This is the ground seed of the same plant that gives us cilantro leaves, but the flavor of each part is distinctly different. Ground coriander adds wonderful aroma and tastes like a lemon-caraway-sage blend. Ground coriander is available in the spice racks of most grocery stores.

**Daikon Radish** (white radish). These long white radishes, 6 to 12 inches long, are mild and sweet.

**Dipping Sauce.** While many types of sauce can be used to dip wontons, egg rolls and lettuce bundles and other items, the term, *dipping sauce* usually refers to a thin mixture with soy sauce or oil and seasonings. You can use plain soy sauce or make easy recipes such as Lemon Dipping Sauce (page 120) with Lime or Orange variations, Horseradish Dipping Sauce (page 121) or Cilantro Dipping Sauce (page 120).

**Duck Sauce** (duk sauce or plum sauce). A sweet-and-sour sauce made from plums. The name comes from the Chinese word for plum and the sauce has nothing to do with game birds. Purchased duck or duk sauces are available in grocery and gourmet shops. To make your own, see page 122 for Sweet-and-Sour Plum Sauce or Sweet-Hot Plum Sauce.

**Egg Roll Skins.** These paper-thin, soft square sheets of dough made from eggs, flour and water are used for wrapping meat, shrimp or vegetables. The stuffed bundles are then deep-fried. The sheets are sold frozen or refrigerated. Allow frozen egg roll skins to thaw completely.

**Five-Spice Powder** (five spices, five-flavored powder, five-fragrance spice powder or five-fragrance powder). This ground mixture of cinnamon, cloves, fennel seed, star anise and Sichuan peppercorns adds a pungent, slightly sweet flavor. It is available in jars or bags on the spice shelves of major grocery stores, food cooperatives and Asian markets. Store, tightly covered, in a dry place at room temperature. To make your own blend, place 3/4 teaspoon whole cloves, 1 1/4 teaspoons whole black peppercorns, 2 teaspoons fennel seed, 4 star anise, broken, and 4 inches of stick cinnamon, broken, in a small blender, a food processor container or a coffee grinder. Blend or grind until powdered.

**Ginger, Ground.** Not a substitute for fresh gingerroot, this dried and ground form of the root has a very different flavor, as found in gingerbread or gingersnap cookies.

**Gingerroot.** This gnarled brown-skinned root tastes peppery and slightly sweet and can be found in the produce section of most grocery stores. Gingerroot can be stored several ways. *To use within 10 days*, store it unpeeled in the crisper section of the refrigerator. Peel and slice or finely shred to use. *To use as slices within 1 month*, place peeled slices in enough sherry to cover; store covered in refrigerator. The sherry will develop a subtle gingerroot flavor, and can also be used for cooking. *To use up to 3 months for grating*, freeze unpeeled roots in a tightly sealed plastic bag. Scrape off peel and grate amount needed; return root to freezer.

**Gingerroot Juice.** Place thin slices of fresh gingerroot in a garlic press to extract juice. Or, squeeze finely chopped gingerroot between fingers to extract the juice. You can substitute ginger-flavored sherry (see **Gingerroot**) or the liquid from **pickled gingerroot** in recipes that are savory rather than sweet.

**Gingerroot, Pickled.** Sold in jars, tender, young or spring gingerroot is preserved in a sweet vinegar sauce and is available in large stores or Asian markets. Or you can make your own (see page 127). Look for smooth, tight and thin-skinned young ginger to make pickled gingerroot. Both the slices and the pickling juice are used in recipes. Store slices, covered with juice, in the refrigerator.

**Hoisin Sauce.** A sweet, moderately-spicy, thick reddish-brown sauce made from soybeans, vinegar, chilies, spices and garlic. It is used in cooking and as a table condiment. Hoisin sauce adds body when used as an ingredient in other sauces. There is no substitute.

**Jicama.** This brown-skinned root vegetable has a crunchy, sweet white interior. It will keep in the refrigerator for several weeks. Water chestnuts can be substituted in salads.

**Lotus Root.** Available fresh and canned in Oriental specialty stores, lotus root is a long potato-like root vegetable with a creamy colored interior. Refrigerate both fresh and canned after opening. There is no substitute.

**Mushrooms, Dried Black** (Chinese dried mushrooms, dried forest mushrooms, dried shiitake mushrooms, winter mushrooms). The Chinese have traditionally used a dried version of the fresh shiitake mushroom that is used in Japanese cooking. With intense mushroom flavor, these have caps that vary in width from 1/2 to 2 inches. They must be soaked in water until tender, then rinsed free of grit before using. Store dried mushrooms tightly covered at room temperature. Fresh mushrooms or straw mushrooms may be substituted in stir-fry recipes only.

**Mushrooms, Straw** (grass mushrooms). These tender mushrooms, about 1 1/2 to 2 inches tall with long leaflike caps, are sold fresh, canned or dried. Soak the dried mushrooms and wash many times in water before using. After opening, store canned mushrooms covered with water.

**Mushrooms, Wood Ear** (cloud ear mushrooms or tree ear mushrooms). These mushrooms are noted for their crunchy character and are used to add texture to dishes.

**Mustard, Chinese Hot** (hot Chinese mustard sauce or mustard sauce). A very hot dipping sauce. It is sold in jars in many grocery stores. It is easy to make your own; see Hot Mustard Sauce (page 123) or Lime-Mustard Sauce (page 123).

**Noodles, Cellophane** (bean threads, glass noodles, vermicelli or transparent noodles). These brittle white noodles made from mung beans become translucent, soft and gelatinous when they absorb liquid or puffy and crisp when deep-fried. They are sold in cellophane packages. Fried rice stick noodles may be substituted for fried cellophane noodles.

*Cooking cellophane noodles: Soak in boiling water just 3 to 5 minutes until they become soft, glassy strands. If, instead, this same noodle is broken and dropped into oil heated to 375°, it puffs to three times its original size and turns white in a few seconds. Rice sticks can be substituted for cellophane noodles.*

**Noodles, Chinese.** Noodles, or *mein* in Chinese, are made of either wheat flour, rice flour or bean starch. Wheat noodles can be made with or without eggs. A mixture of wheat flour and water, Chinese noodles are flat or round. The thin round noodles, sometimes called **Chinese Vermicelli,** are most similar to Italian pasta such as angel hair or thin spaghetti. When found fresh in the produce case of major grocery stores or Asian markets, they may be labeled **Stir-fry Noodles** or simply **Fresh Chinese Noodles.** When these noodles are cooked in stir-fry sauce they are called **Lo Mein** noodles, and are sometimes frozen with a sauce packet.

*Cooking Chinese and egg noodles: Dried noodles must be steamed or boiled before cooking in a stir-fry sauce. Vegetables can be parboiled along with the noodles. See Easy Two-Pan Lo Mein (page 105). Fresh noodles can be cooked directly in the stir-fry sauce. See Smoked Turkey Lo Mein (page 51). Italian pasta can be substituted for Asian pasta. A pound of dried noodles produces 5 cups cooked noodles. A pound of fresh noodles produces 2 1/2 cups cooked noodles.*

**Noodles, Chow Mein.** These are Chinese noodles which have been soft-fried in oil until crisp and are, therefore, high in fat.

**Noodles, Egg.** Made of flour, water and eggs, these noodles are served pan-fried or in soups and are available dried, fresh or frozen. Thin, cholesterol-free noodles are the preferred substitute

for flat Chinese egg noodles, and spaghetti is a good substitute for the round ones. See **Noodles, Chinese** for cooking information.

**Noodles, Rice Stick** (long rice, rice flour noodles or rice vermicelli). These thin, brittle white noodles made from rice powder must be softened in liquid before stir-frying. When deep-fried they become puffy and crisp and are used as a garnish. Rice sticks are sold in cellophane packages and stored at room temperature. Deep-fried cellophane noodles may be substituted for deep-fried rice stick noodles. When soaked, they hold their shape better and have a firmer texture than cellophane noodles.

*Cooking rice sticks: Soak in boiling water for 10 minutes if adding to a stir-fry mixture. Boil 3 minutes if using as plain noodle. Deep-fat fry at 375° 10 seconds for crispy puffed noodles.*

**Oyster Sauce.** The rich flavor of this thick brown sauce comes from cooking oyster extract with dark soy sauce for a subtle seafood flavor. Hoisin sauce can be substituted.

**Rice.** There are two principal varieties of rice: long grain and short grain. Long grain rice is generally preferred for Chinese cooking because it is firmer when cooked. It should be washed in cold water until the water is clear to remove excess starch. Store uncooked rice at room temperature.

**Rice, Long Grain White.** The basic rice of Chinese cooking. One cup of uncooked long grain rice makes 3 cups cooked rice. Rice can be boiled, steamed or cooked in an electric rice cooker. It is the Chinese custom to rinse rice 5 or 6 times in large quantities of water before cooking to remove excess starch. The result is fresh tasting, light-textured rice which does not clump together. Do not eliminate the rinsing process if you are using an electric rice cooker; the rice will boil over. White rice can be kept warm for up to 20 minutes if left in the saucepan, covered and removed from the heat. Or cook ahead of time and refrigerate; reheat in the microwave or by steaming (see page 7).

*Cooking white rice: Place 2 cups long grain white rice in 2-quart saucepan. Add enough cold water to cover rice. Wash rice by rubbing rice gently between fingers; drain. Repeat 5 or 6 times until water runs clear; drain. Add 1 cup cold water and 1/2 teaspoon salt, if desired; heat to boiling. Cover tightly; reduce heat and simmer 20 minutes or until liquid is absorbed. 6 cups.*

**Rice, Fried.** Made from cold, cooked rice. Usually seasoned with soy sauce, the rice is stir-fried with bits of vegetables or meats and egg. It is not the Chinese custom to serve fried rice as a side dish or accompaniment to main dishes as it is often served here. Our Oven-Fried Rice (page 102) uses less fat than rice stir-fried in oil.

**Rice, Glutinous** (sweet rice, sticky rice). A short grain, opaque rice which is used for meatballs, puddings or stuffing. It is coated with glucose and produces a sticky rice. It can be boiled or steamed. Steaming takes longer but the rice cannot burn.

*Steaming glutinous rice: Place 1 cup glutinous (sweet) rice in medium bowl; cover with cold water. Let stand 3 hours or overnight; drain and rinse. Spread rice in thin, even layer in colander, sieve or steamer basket lined with cheesecloth. Steam, covered, over rapidly boiling water 25 minutes. Sprinkle with 1/4 teaspoon salt, if desired. Steam 20 to 25 minutes longer, or until tender and translucent. Add extra boiling water to steamer pan if necessary. 2 cups.*

**Rices, Other. Parboiled Rice** has been steamed to reduce the cooking time. The cooked rice is more fluffy, separate and harder to eat with chopsticks. The package may say "instant" or "converted" rice. **Brown Rice** has not had the bran layer removed, so it has more protein, calcium, phosphorous, potassium, niacin and vitamin E. Brown rice requires more water, 2 1/2 cups to 1 cup rice, and more time to cook (45 minutes). It remains firmer and has a nutty flavor which is enhanced by toasting before boiling. As it can turn rancid from the oil in the bran, use brown rice within 6 months. **Instant Brown Rice** has been parboiled to cook in 15 minutes or less. Several rices, such as Jasmine and Basmati, are valued for their fragrant aroma as well as their nut-like flavor. **Jasmine** is an aromatic Thai rice. **Basmati** is an aged Indian or Pakistani rice.

**Sesame Oil.** Because this oil is formed by pressing sesame seeds, it has a delightful, nutty flavor. It can be found in both dark and light varieties. Dark **Toasted Sesame Oil**, made from toasted sesame seeds, has the most intense and distinctive flavor and aroma. Look for sesame oil in Asian markets, gourmet shops or in the Oriental foods section of major grocery stores. Store in a cool place away from sunlight up to 1 month or refrigerate for up to 1 year.

**Sherry.** Sherry is a fortified wine. Cooking sherry, sold in grocery stores, has salt added. Better tasting sherries, without salt, are sold in liquor stores. Japanese rice wine (mirin) or sake could also be used. Store at room temperature away from direct sunlight. Non-alcoholic dry white wine or fat-free chicken broth can be substituted.

**Siu Mai Skins.** These are thin, soft 3 1/2-inch circles of dough made from eggs, flour and water. They are used for dumplings and filled with meat, poultry or seafood mixtures to be steamed or boiled. Wonton skins can be substituted; remove the corners to form circles. Siu mai skins are sold frozen or refrigerated.

**Soy Sauce.** This salty brown sauce is made from soybeans, wheat, yeast and salt. There are three types: light, dark and heavy. **Light Soy Sauce**—light in color and delicately flavored—is used in clear soups and in marinades. **Lite Soy Sauce** is a reduced-sodium soy sauce. Since you often must use twice as much of lite soy (with 200mg of sodium per teaspoon) to equal the flavor of regular soy sauce (with 320mg of sodium per teaspoon) we have not used lite soy sauce in these recipes. **Dark Soy Sauce** is made from the same ingredients as light, with the addition of caramel for a richer color. Both light and dark soy sauces can be used as table condiments. **Heavy or Sweet Soy Sauce** is made with molasses and is thick and dark. It is used for color in dark sauces. **Tamari** is a soy sauce made without wheat.

**Soy Sauce, Mushroom.** This soy sauce is flavored with mushrooms and a hint of sugar. It is dark and slightly thicker than regular soy sauce, delicious when added to stir-fried meat or vegetable dishes.

**Spring Roll Skins.** These paper-thin, translucent squares or rounds of dough are similar to egg roll skins. They are sold frozen or refrigerated. Egg roll skins may be substituted, although they have a different texture.

**Stir-fry Sauce.** A thickened, seasoned soy sauce used in stir-fry cooking. Available ready-made in a variety of flavors, stir-fry sauces vary greatly in quality but have greatly improved in the last few years. Find a favorite brand and use it when time is short. To make your own, see page 124 for Garlic Stir-Fry Sauce.

**Sweet-and-Sour Sauce.** Any sauce with sugar, fruit juices, honey or other sweeteners as well as vinegar or citrus juices might be called a sweet-and-sour sauce. Besides those commercially available, see the recipes for Chinese Lemon Sauce (page 121), Sweet-and-Sour Plum Sauce (page 122), Hot-Sweet Apricot Mustard (page 123) and Orange-Ginger Sauce (page 122).

**Sichuan Sauce** (Szechuan sauce or Szechwan sauce). A relatively thin, hot sauce with soy sauce, chilies, garlic and gingerroot. Purchased Sichuan sauces can have as much variety in level of heat as there are spellings of the name. To make your own Easy Sichuan Sauce, see page 124.

**Tofu** (bean curd, dou fu, soybean curd or bean cake). A bland, smooth, custard-like mixture made from pureed soybeans, tofu readily absorbs the flavors it's cooked in. It is fragile, requires little or no cooking, and is a good and inexpensive source of vegetable protein. **Lite Firm Tofu** has 88% less fat that regular firm tofu. Look for firm or extra firm varieties for stir-frying, as these hold up better than the soft variety. Follow package directions for storing unopened packages. Any partial cakes must be refrigerated covered with water and tightly covered; change water daily.

**Vinegar, Chinese Black** (red vinegar). A tangy dark vinegar from Zhejiang province. Italian balsamic vinegar is the closest substitution.

**Vinegar, Rice.** A mild, light-golden to clear colored vinegar found in most grocery stores and Asian markets. It has a fresh, light taste which is important to Chinese cooking. Store at room temperature away from direct sunlight. **Seasoned Rice Vinegar** has salt, sugar and MSG added.

**Water Chestnuts.** The crisp, white, delicately flavored bulb of an Asian marsh plant, the water chestnut is used as a vegetable for stir-frying and in soups and cold dishes. Fresh water chestnuts must be washed and peeled before using; canned, they are ready to eat. Peeled jicama may be substituted.

**Wonton Skins.** These thin, soft 3 1/2-inch squares of dough are made from eggs, flour and water. They are filled with meat, vegetable or seafood mixtures, then deep-fried, boiled or steamed. The corners can be removed and the rounds used for dumplings. They are sold frozen or refrigerated. Egg roll skins, cut into quarters, may be substituted.

# METRIC CONVERSION GUIDE

## VOLUME

| U.S. Units | Canadian Metric | Australian Metric |
|---|---|---|
| 1/4 teaspoon | 1 mL | 1 ml |
| 1/2 teaspoon | 2 mL | 2 ml |
| 1 teaspoon | 5 mL | 5 ml |
| 1 tablespoon | 15 mL | 20 ml |
| 1/4 cup | 50 mL | 60 ml |
| 1/3 cup | 75 mL | 80 ml |
| 1/2 cup | 125 mL | 125 ml |
| 2/3 cup | 150 mL | 170 ml |
| 3/4 cup | 175 mL | 190 ml |
| 1 cup | 250 mL | 250 ml |
| 1 quart | 1 liter | 1 liter |
| 1 1/2 quarts | 1.5 liters | 1.5 liters |
| 2 quarts | 2 liters | 2 liters |
| 2 1/2 quarts | 2.5 liters | 2.5 liters |
| 3 quarts | 3 liters | 3 liters |
| 4 quarts | 4 liters | 4 liters |

## WEIGHT

| U.S. Units | Canadian Metric | Australian Metric |
|---|---|---|
| 1 ounce | 30 grams | 30 grams |
| 2 ounces | 55 grams | 60 grams |
| 3 ounces | 85 grams | 90 grams |
| 4 ounces (1/4 pound) | 115 grams | 125 grams |
| 8 ounces (1/2 pound) | 225 grams | 225 grams |
| 16 ounces (1 pound) | 455 grams | 500 grams |
| 1 pound | 455 grams | 1/2 kilogram |

**Note:** The recipes in this cookbook have not been developed or tested using metric measures. When converting recipes to metric, some variations in quality may be noted.

## MEASUREMENTS

| Inches | Centimeters |
|---|---|
| 1 | 2.5 |
| 2 | 5.0 |
| 3 | 7.5 |
| 4 | 10.0 |
| 5 | 12.5 |
| 6 | 15.0 |
| 7 | 17.5 |
| 8 | 20.5 |
| 9 | 23.0 |
| 10 | 25.5 |
| 11 | 28.0 |
| 12 | 30.5 |
| 13 | 33.0 |
| 14 | 35.5 |
| 15 | 38.0 |

## TEMPERATURES

| Fahrenheit | Celsius |
|---|---|
| 32° | 0° |
| 212° | 100° |
| 250° | 120° |
| 275° | 140° |
| 300° | 150° |
| 325° | 160° |
| 350° | 180° |
| 375° | 190° |
| 400° | 200° |
| 425° | 220° |
| 450° | 230° |
| 475° | 240° |
| 500° | 260° |

# HELPFUL NUTRITION AND COOKING INFORMATION

## NUTRITION GUIDELINES:

We provide nutrition information for each recipe that includes calories, fat, cholesterol, sodium, carbohydrate, fiber and protein. Vitamin, mineral and protein amounts are also listed. Individual food choices can be based on this information.

Daily Values are set by the Food and Drug Administration and are based on the needs of most healthy adults. Percent Daily Values are based on an average diet of 2,000 calories per day. Your daily values may be higher or lower depending on your calorie needs.

**Recommended intake for a daily diet of 2,000 calories as set by the Food and Drug Administration:**

| | |
|---|---|
| Total Fat | Less than 65 g |
| Saturated Fat | Less than 20g |
| Cholesterol | Less than 300mg |
| Sodium | Less than 2,400mg |
| Total Carbohydrate | 300g |
| Dietary Fiber | 25g |

Dietary exchange information is based on criteria set by the American Dietetic Association and the American Diabetes Association.

## CRITERIA USED FOR CALCULATING NUTRITION INFORMATION:

- The first ingredient is used wherever a choice is given (such as 1/3 cup sour cream or plain yogurt).

- The first ingredient amount is used wherever a range is given (such as 3 to 3 1/2 pounds cut-up broiler-fryer chicken).

- The first serving number is used wherever a range is given (such as 4 to 6 servings).

- "If desired" ingredients such as "sprinkle with brown sugar if desired" and recipe variations are *not* included.

- Only the amount of a marinade that is estimated to be absorbed by the food during preparation or cooking was calculated.

- White rice was used wherever cooked rice is listed in the ingredients, unless otherwise indicated.

- Cooked rice, pasta or vegetables are unsalted when called for as an ingredient.

## COOKING TERMS GLOSSARY:

Cooking has its own vocabulary just like many other creative activities. Here are some basic cooking terms to use as a handy reference.

**Beat:** Mix ingredients vigorously with spoon, fork, wire whisk, hand beater or electric mixer until smooth and uniform.

**Blend:** Mix ingredients with spoon, wire whisk or rubber scraper, until very smooth and uniform. A blender, hand blender or food processor can be used.

**Boil:** Heat liquid until bubbles rise continuously and break on the surface and steam is given off. For rolling boil, the bubbles form rapidly.

**Chop:** Cut into coarse or fine irregular pieces with a knife, food chopper, blender or food processor.

**Crisp-tender:** Doneness description of vegetables cooked until tender but still retaining some of the crisp texture of the raw food.

**Cube:** Cut into squares 1/2 inch or larger.

**Dice:** Cut into squares smaller than 1/2 inch.

**Grate:** Cut into tiny particles using small rough holes of grater (citrus peel or chocolate).

**Grease:** Rub the inside surface of a pan with shortening, using pastry brush, piece of waxed paper or paper towel, to prevent food from sticking during baking (as for some casseroles).

**Julienne:** Cut into thin, matchlike strips, using knife or food processor (vegetables, fruits, meats).

**Mix:** Combine ingredients in any way that distributes them evenly.

**Sauté:** Cook foods in hot oil or margarine over medium-high heat with frequent tossing and turning motion.

**Shred:** Cut into long thin pieces by rubbing food across the holes of a shredder, as for cheese, or by using a knife to slice very thinly, as for cabbage.

**Simmer:** Cook in liquid just below the boiling point on top of the stove; usually after reducing heat from a boil. Bubbles will rise slowly and break just below the surface.

**Stir:** Mix ingredients until uniform consistency. Stir once in a while for stirring occasionally, often for stirring frequently and continuously for stirring constantly.

**Toss:** Tumble ingredients lightly with a lifting motion (such as green salad), usually to coat evenly or mix with another food.

## Ingredients Used in Recipe Testing:

- Ingredients used for testing represent those that the majority of consumers use in their homes: large eggs, canned ready-to-use chicken broth, and vegetable oil spread containing *not less than 65% fat.*

- Fat-free, low-fat or low-sodium products are not used, unless otherwise indicated.

- Solid vegetable shortening (not butter, margarine, nonstick cooking sprays or vegetable oil spread as they can cause sticking problems) is used to grease pans, unless otherwise indicated.

## Equipment Used in Recipe Testing:

We use equipment for testing that the majority of consumers use in their homes. If a specific piece of equipment (such as a wire whisk) is necessary for recipe success, it will be listed in the recipe.

- No black or insulated bakeware was used.

- When a baking *pan* is specified in a recipe, a *metal* pan was used; a baking *dish* or pie *plate* means oven-proof glass was used.

- An electric hand mixer is used for mixing *only when mixer speeds are specified* in the recipe directions. When a mixer speed is not given, a spoon or fork was used.

# INDEX

Numbers in *italics* refer to photos.

**65**POINTS

**SAVE** these Betty Crocker Points and redeem them for big savings on hundreds of kitchen, home, gift and children's items! For catalog, send 50¢ with your name and address to: General Mills, P.O. Box 5389, Mpls., MN 55460.

Redeemable with cash in USA before May 1999. Void where prohibited, taxed or regulated.

S

CUT OUT AND SAVE